IMPROVE
YOUR
MEMORY

IMPROVE **YOUR** MEMORY

FOURTH EDITION

BY **RON FRY**

CAREER PRESS
Franklin Lakes, NJ

IMPROVE YOUR MEMORY, 4TH EDITION
Cover design by Design Solutions
Printed in the U.S.A. by Book-mart Press

To order this title, please call toll-free 1-800-CAREER-1 (NJ and Canada: 201-848-0310) to order using VISA or MasterCard, or for further information on books from Career Press.

CAREER
PRESS

The Career Press, Inc., 3 Tice Road, PO Box 687,
Franklin Lakes, NJ 07417
www.careerpress.com

Library of Congress Cataloging-in-Publication Data

Fry, Ronald W.
      Improve your memory / by Ron Fry.—4th ed.
          p.   cm.
      Includes index.
      ISBN 1-56414-459-3 (paper)
      1. Mnemonics. 2. Memory. I. Title.

BF385 F79 2000
153.1'4—dc21   00-031196

Contents

Something to Remember

HIS YEAR MARKS another major milestone in the decade-long evolution of my *How to Study Program*—the reissuance of new editions of the key volumes: *How to Study* itself, now in a fifth edition; fourth editions of *Improve Your Memory, Improve Your Reading, Improve Your Writing,* and *"Ace" Any Test*; and a second edition of *Get Organized*. (*Take Notes, Manage Your Time,* and *Use Your Computer*, though still available, were not revised this year.)

I am truly proud, though somewhat amazed, that *How to Study* itself is now well into its second decade. While all authors want to believe their books will last forever, most wind up in the remainder bin far sooner than we would ever like (or admit).

Why are these books the best-selling series of study guides ever published? Why are they still so *needed*, not only by students but by their parents, who want so badly for them to do well? Because virtually all of the conditions I've been writing and speaking about across the country since 1988 have remained...or gotten *worse:*

1. Despite modest recent improvements in test scores, U.S. students still score abysmally low compared to many other countries, especially on science and math tests.

2. Most parents, when polled, say improving our public schools is our nation's number one priority. Those same parents do *not* think public schools are doing a very good job teaching their kids much of anything.

3. Business leaders continue to complain that far too many entry-level job candidates can barely read, write, add, or multiply. Many can't fill out job applications! As a result, businesses are spending billions to teach employees the basic skills everyone agrees they should have learned in school.

It's almost inevitable that these conditions will *continue to worsen*. This means that the old problems that most affect students' ability to learn—overcrowded classrooms, lack of resources (especially computers and other new technologies), lack of qualified teachers—will continue to frustrate students who want to learn but need help.

As a result, the need for the books in my *How to Study Program* will, unfortunately, continue, since they offer *exactly* the help most students need and their parents demand.

So who are you?

A number of you are students, not just the high school students I always thought were my readers, but also college students (a rousing plug for their high school preparation) and _junior_ high school students (which says something far more positive about their motivation and eventual success).

Many of you are adults returning to school, and some of you are long out of school, but if you could learn _now_ the study skills your teachers never taught you, you would do better in your careers—especially if you knew how to recall the key points you'll need to make in your presentation or remember the new clients' names.

All too many of you are parents with the same lament: "How do I get Jill to do better in school? She can't remember my birthday, let alone when her next trigonometry test is."

I want to briefly take the time to address every one of the audiences for this book and discuss some of the factors particular to each of you:

If you're a high school student

You should be particularly comfortable with both the language and format of this book—its relatively short sentences and paragraphs, occasionally humorous (hopefully) headings and subheadings, a reasonable but certainly not outrageous vocabulary. I wrote it with you in mind!

If you're a junior high school student

It doesn't do much good to figure out how to study if you can't remember anything that you've just read, so learning to improve your memory is definitely key. You are trying to learn how to study at _precisely_ the right time. Sixth, 7th, and 8th grades—before that sometimes-cosmic leap to high school—are without a doubt the period in which all these study skills should be mastered. If you're serious enough about studying to be reading this book, I doubt you'll have trouble with the concepts or the language.

If you're a "traditional" college student...

...somewhere in the 18 to 25 age range, I would have hoped you had already learned all of the study techniques, especially basic memory techniques. If not (and even if you know some tips but not every trick and gimmick covered in this book), I guarantee that truly mastering these memory techniques will help you long after you graduate (with A's, of course!).

If you're the parent of a student of any age

Your child's school is probably doing little if anything to teach him or her how to study. Which means he or she is not learning how to *learn*. And that means he or she is not learning how to *succeed*.

Should the schools be accomplishing that? Absolutely. After all, we spend $275 billion on elementary and secondary education in this country, *an average of $6,000 per student per year*. We ought to be getting more for that money than possible graduation, some football cheers, and a yearbook.

What can parents do?

There are probably even more dedicated parents out there than dedicated students, because the first phone call at any of my radio or TV appearances usually comes from a sincere and worried parent asking, "What can I do to help my kid do better in school?" Okay, here they are, the rules for parents of students of any age:

1. **Set up a homework area.** Free of distraction, well-lit, all necessary supplies handy.

2. **Set up a homework routine.** When and where it gets done. Same time, same place, every day.

3. **Set homework priorities.** Actually, just make the point that homework *is* the priority — before a date, before TV, before going out to play, before whatever.

4. **Make reading a habit** — for them, certainly, but also for yourselves, presuming it isn't already. Kids will inevitably do what you *do*, not what you *say* (even if you say *not* to do what you *do*). So if you keep nagging them to read while *you* turn on the eighth sitcom of the night, what message do you think you're giving them?

5. **Turn off the TV.** Or, at the very least, severely limit when and how much TV-watching is appropriate. This may be the toughest one. Believe me, I'm the father of an 11-year-old. I know. Do your best.

6. **Talk to the teachers.** Find out what your kids are supposed to be learning. If you don't, you can't really supervise. You might even be teaching them things at odds with what the teacher's trying to do.

7. **Encourage and motivate**, but don't nag them to do their homework. It doesn't work.

8. **Supervise their work**, but don't fall into the trap of *doing* their homework for them.

9. **Praise them to succeed**, but don't overpraise them for mediocre work. Kids know when you're slinging it. Be wary of any school or teacher that is more worried about your kid's "self esteem" than her grades, skills, and abilities. I'm not advocating the withdrawal of kudos for good work, but kids need to get the message that "you get what you pay for"; that

you need to work hard to actually *earn* rewards. Horror stories about teachers giving out good grades, reducing standards, or not assigning homework because they're afraid some of the kids will "feel bad" if they don't do well are exactly that—horrible, scary stories. Such tactics merely set kids up for *bigger* failures down the road in a world that will put a premium on their skills and abilities and not care very much how they "feel" about it.

10. **Convince them of reality.** (This is for older students.) Okay, I'll admit it's almost as much of a stretch as turning off the TV, but learning and believing that the real world will not care about their grades but measure them solely by what they know and what they can do is a lesson that will save many tears (probably yours). It's probably never too early to (carefully) let your boy or girl genius get the message that life is not fair. Which is why teaching them resilience and determination—so they'll pick themselves up, dust themselves off, and try again when they fail— is paramount.

11. **If you can afford it, get your kid(s) a computer** and all the software they can handle. Many people have been saying it for years (including me) and there really is no avoiding it: Your kids, whatever their age, absolutely must master technology (computers) in order to survive, let alone succeed, in and after school. There's even new empirical data to back up all the braying: A recent decade-long study has shown that kids who master computers learn faster and earn higher test scores.

12. **Turn off the TV already!**

13. **Get wired.** The Internet is the greatest invention of our age and an unbelievable tool for students of any age. While it's impossible to list even a smattering of helpful sites in a book this brief, parents of elementary and high school students should check out the following:

www.schoolwork.org

www.sunsite.berkeley.edu/KidsClick

www.HomeworkCentral.com

   (a division of *www.bigchalk.com*)

www.iln.net

www.tutor.com

The importance of your involvement

Don't for a minute underestimate the importance of *your* commitment to your child's success: Your involvement in your child's education is absolutely essential to his or her eventual success.

Surprisingly enough, the results of every study done in the last three decades about what affects a child's success in school clearly demonstrate that only one factor *overwhelmingly* affects it, every time: parental involvement. Not the size of the school, the money spent per pupil, the number of language labs, how many of the students go on to college, how many great teachers there are (or lousy ones). All factors, yes. *But none as significant as the effect you can have.*

So please, take the time to read this book (and all of the others in the series, but especially *How to Study*) yourself. Learn what your kids *should* be learning (and which of the other subject-specific books in the series your child needs the most).

And you can help tremendously, *even if you were not a great student yourself, even if you never learned great study skills.*

You can learn now with your child — not only will it help him or her in school, it will help *you* on the job, whatever your field.

If you're a nontraditional student

If you're going back to high school, college, or graduate school at age 25, 45, 65, or 85 — you probably need the help my books offer more than anyone! Why? Because the longer you've been out of school, the more likely you don't remember what you've forgotten. And you've probably forgotten what you're supposed to remember! As much as I emphasize that it's rarely too early to learn good study habits, I must also emphasize that it's never too *late*.

If you're returning to school and attempting to carry even a partial load of courses while simultaneously holding down a job, raising a family, or both, there are some particular problems you face that you probably didn't the first time you were in school:

Time and money pressures. Let's face it, when all you had to worry about was going to school, it simply *had* to be easier than going to school, raising a family, and working for a living simultaneously. (And it was!) Mastering all of the techniques of time management is even more essential if you are to effectively juggle your many responsibilities to your career, family, clubs, friends, and so forth with your commitment to school. Money management may well be another essential skill, whether figuring out how to pay for childcare (something you probably didn't have to worry about the last time you were in school) or how to manage all your responsibilities while cutting your hours at work to make time for school.

Self-imposed fears of inadequacy. You may well convince yourself that you're just "out of practice" with all this school stuff. You don't even remember what to do with a highlighter! While some of this fear is valid, most is not.

The valid part is that you are returning to an academic atmosphere, one that you may not have even visited for a decade or two. And it *is* different (which I'll discuss more in the following paragraphs) than the "work-a-day" world. That's just a matter of adjustment and, trust me, it will take a matter of days, if not hours, to dissipate. But I suspect what many of you are really fearing is that you just aren't in that school "mentality" anymore, that you don't "think" the same way. Or, perhaps more pertinently to this book, that the skills you need to succeed in school are rusty.

I think these last fears are groundless. You've been out there thinking and doing for quite a few years, perhaps very successfully, so it's really ridiculous to think school will be so different. It won't be. Relax. And while you may think your study skills are rusty, you've probably been using them every day in your career without even realizing it. Even if I can't convince you, you have my *How to Study Program*, your refresher course. It will probably teach you more about studying than you ever forgot.

Maybe you're worried because you didn't exactly light up the academic power plant the first time around. Well, neither did Edison, Einstein, or a host of other relatively successful people. But then, you've changed rather significantly since then, haven't you? Held a series of jobs, raised a family, saved money, taken on more and more responsibility? Concentrate on how much *more* qualified you are for school *now* than you were then!

Feeling you're "out of your element." This is a slightly different fear, the fear that you just don't fit in any more. After all, you're not 18 again. But then, neither are fully half the college students on campuses today. That's right, fully 50 percent of all college students are older than 25. The reality is, you'll probably feel more in your element now than you did the first time around!

You'll see teachers differently. Probably a plus. It's doubtful you'll have the same awe you did the first time around. At worst, you'll consider teachers your equals. At best, you'll consider them younger and not necessarily as successful or experienced as you are. In either event, you probably won't be quite as ready to treat your college professors as if they were omnipotent.

There *are* differences in academic life. It's slower than the "real" world, and you may well be moving significantly faster than its normal pace. When you were 18, an afternoon without classes meant a game of Frisbee. Now it might mean catching up on a week's worth of errands, cooking (and freezing) a week's worth of dinners, and/or writing four reports due last week. Despite your own hectic schedule, do not expect campus life to accelerate in response. You will have to get used to people and systems with far less interest in speed.

Some random thoughts about learning

Learning shouldn't be painful and certainly doesn't have to be boring, though it's far too often both. However, it's not necessarily going to be wonderful and painless, either. Sometimes you actually have to work hard to figure something out or get a project done. That *is* reality.

It's also reality that everything isn't readily apparent or easily understandable. Confusion reigns. Tell yourself that's okay and learn how to get past it. Heck, if you actually think you're supposed to understand everything you read the first time through, you're kidding yourself. Learning something slowly doesn't mean there's something wrong with you. It may be a subject that virtually everybody learns slowly.

A good student doesn't panic when something doesn't seem to be getting through the haze. He just takes his time, follows whatever steps apply, and remains confident that the light bulb will indeed inevitably go on.

Parents often ask me, "How can I motivate my teen-ager?" My initial response is usually to say, "If I knew the answer to that question, I would have retired very wealthy quite some time ago." However, I think there *is* an answer, but it's not something *parents* can do—it's something you, the student, have to decide: Are you going to spend the school day interested and alert or bored and resentful?

It's really that simple. Why not develop the attitude that you have to go to school anyway, so rather than being bored or miserable while you're there, you might as well be active and learn as much as possible? The difference between a C and an A or B for many students is, I firmly believe, merely a matter of wanting to do better. As I constantly stress in interviews, inevitably you will leave school. And very quickly, you'll discover the premium is on what you know and what you can do. Grades won't count anymore, and neither will tests. So you can learn it all now or regret it later.

How many times have you said to yourself, "I don't know why I'm bothering trying to learn this calculus (or algebra, geometry, physics, chemistry, history, whatever), I'll *never* use this again!"? I hate to burst bubbles, but unless you've got a patent on some great new fortune-telling device, you have *no clue* what you're going to need to know tomorrow or next week, let alone next year or in a decade.

I've been amazed in my own life how things I did with no specific purpose in mind (except probably to earn money) turned out years later to be not just invaluable to my life or career, but essential. How was I to know when I took German as my language elective in high school that the most important international trade show in book publishing, my field, was in Frankfurt...Germany? Or that the basic skills I learned one year working for an accountant (while I was writing my first book) would become essential when I later started four companies? Or how important basic math skills would be in selling and negotiating over the years? (Okay, I'll admit it: I haven't used a differential equation in 20 years, but, hey, you never know!)

So learn it *all*. And don't be surprised if the subject you'd vote "least likely to ever be useful" winds up being the key to *your* fame and fortune.

There *are* other study guides

Though I immodestly maintain my *How to Study Program* to be the most helpful to the most people, there are certainly lots of other purported study books out there. Unfortunately, I don't think many of them deliver what they promise. In fact, I'm actually getting mad at the growing number of study guides out there claiming to be "the sure way to straight A's" or something of the sort. These are also the books that dismiss reasonable alternative ways to study and learn with, "Well, that never worked for me," as if that is a valid reason to dismiss it, as if we should *care* that it didn't work for the author.

Inevitably, these books promote the authors' "system," which usually means what *they* did to get through school.

This "system," whether basic and traditional or wildly quirky, may or may not work for you. So what do you do if "their" way of taking notes makes no sense to you? Or you master their highfalutin' "Super Student Study Symbols" and still get C's?

I'm not getting into a Dennis Miller rant here, but there are very few "rights" and "wrongs" out there in the study world. There's certainly no single "right" way to attack a multiple choice test or absolute "right" way to take notes. So don't get fooled into thinking there *is*, especially if what you're doing seems to be working for you.

Don't change what ain't broke because some self-proclaimed study guru claims what you're doing is all wet.

Maybe he's all wet. After all, if his system works for you, all it *really* means is you have the same likes, dislikes, talents, or skills as the author.

Needless to say, don't read *my* books looking for the Truth — that single, inestimable system of "rules" that works for everyone. You won't find it, 'cause there's no such bird.

You *will* find a plethora of techniques, tips, tricks, gimmicks, and what-have-you, some or all of which may work for you, some of which won't. Pick and choose, change and adapt, figure out what works for you. Because *you* are the one responsible for creating *your* study system, *not me*.

Yes, I'll occasionally point out "my way" of doing something. I may even suggest that I think it offers some clear advantages to all the alternative ways of accomplishing the same thing. But that *doesn't* mean it's some carved-in-stone, deviate-from-the-sacred-Ron-Fry-study-path-under-penalty-of-a-writhing-death kind of rule.

I've used the phrase "study smarter, not harder" as a sort of catch phrase in promotion and publicity for the *How to Study Program* for nearly a decade. So what does it mean to you? Does it mean I guarantee you'll spend less time studying? Or that the least amount of time is best? Or that studying isn't ever supposed to be hard?

Hardly. It means that studying inefficiently is wasting time that could be spent doing other (okay, probably more *fun*) things and that getting your studying done as quickly and efficiently as possible is a realistic, worthy, and *attainable* goal. I'm no stranger to hard work, but I'm not a monastic dropout who thrives on self-flagellation. I try not to work harder than I have to!

What you'll remember from *this* one

If you have trouble remembering your own phone number, this is the book for you. This new edition is even more complete—a simple, practical, easy-to-use memory book that will help you:

- ✎ Remember numbers.
- ✎ Remember dates and facts.
- ✎ Retain more of what you read the *first* time you read it.
- ✎ Take notes that will help you score well on tests and term papers.
- ✎ Remember numbers.
- ✎ Build a bigger vocabulary.
- ✎ Remember how to spell.
- ✎ Remember names and faces.
- ✎ Remember numbers. (I get the feeling this is *everyone's* biggest problem!)

What's more, *Improve Your Memory* will help you do *all* of this without a mind-numbing amount of time and effort. Its advice is easy to learn and even easier to apply.

Along the way, you might even develop the skills for knowing at all times where you've left your glasses, car keys, or wallet.

The best way to approach this book is to read Chapters 1 through 9 straight through, then go back and review some of the mechanics of memory improvement contained in Chapters 3 through 9. If you have ADD—or are the parent of someone who does—be sure to read Chapter 10.

After this review, take the tests in Chapter 11 and see how much you've improved *your* memory. I'm sure you'll be amazed. When you've finished this book, you'll be effortlessly flexing mental muscles you never knew you had!

www.study.com

In 1988, when I wrote the first edition of **How to Study**, I composed it, formatted it, and printed it on (gasp) a personal computer. Yes, boys and girls, in those halycon days, I was surfing a wave that didn't hit shore for a few more years. Most people did *not* have a computer, yet alone a neighborhood network and DSL, or surf the Web (whatever that was), or chat online, or Instant Message their friends, or…you get the point.

In case you've been living in a cave that Bill Gates forgot to wire, those days are very dead and gone. And you should cheer, even if you aren't sure what DOS was (is? could be?). Because the spread of the personal computer and, even more, the Internet, has taken studying from the Dark Ages to the Info Age in merely a decade.

As a result, you will find all of my books assume you have a computer and know how to use it — for note-taking, reading, paper-writing, researching, and much more. There are many tasks that may be harder on a computer — and I'll point them out — but don't believe for a second that a computer won't help you tremendously, whatever your age, whatever your grades.

As for the Internet, it has absolutely revolutionized research. Whether you're writing a paper, putting together a reading list, studying for the SAT, or just trying to organize your life, it has become a more valuable tool than the greatest library in the world. Heck, it *is* the greatest library in the world…and more. So if you are not Internet savvy (yes, I'm talking to the parents out there, couldn't you tell?), admit you're a dummy, get a book (over the Internet, of course) and get wired. You'll be missing far too much — and be studying far harder — without it.

In case you were wondering

Before we get on with all the tips and techniques necessary to remember anything you need to, *when* you need to, let me make two important points about all my study books.

First, I believe in gender equality, in writing as well as in life. Unfortunately, I find constructions such as "he and she," "s/he," "womyn," and other such stretches to be sometimes painfully awkward. I have therefore attempted to sprinkle pronouns of both genders throughout the text.

Second, you will find many pieces of advice, examples, lists, phrases, and sections spread throughout two or more of my books. Certainly *How to Study*, which is an overview of all the study skills, necessarily contains, though in summarized form, some of each of the other books.

The repetition is unavoidable. While I urge everyone to read all the books in the series, but especially *How to Study*, they *are* nine individual books. And many people only buy one of them. Consequently, I must include in each the pertinent material *for that topic*, even if that material is then repeated in a second or even a third book.

That said, I can guarantee that the nearly 1,200 pages of my *How to Study Program* contain the most wide-ranging, comprehensive, and complete system of studying ever published. I have attempted to create a system that is usable, that is useful, that is practical, that is learnable. One that *you* can use—whatever your age, whatever your level of achievement, whatever your IQ—to start doing better in school, in work, and in life *immediately*.

—Ron Fry

May 2000

CHAPTER 1

Thank You, Zbigniew

 HICH DO YOU think you're more likely to remember — your first date with your future spouse (even if it was decades ago) or what you had for breakfast last Thursday morning?

Probably the former (though not if last Thursday was your first experiment with yak butter).

Which event conjures up the most memories — the Blizzard of 1996 or the last time it rained (unless, of course, it *really* poured cats and dogs)?

Which name would you find difficult to forget — Joe Smith or Zbigniew Brzezinski? We'll deal with how to remember *spelling* old Zbig in Chapters 5 and 7.

What do all the "memorable" names, dates, places, and events have in common? The fact that they're *different*. What makes something memorable is its *extra*ordinariness, how much it differs from our normal experiences.

The reason so many of us forget where we put the car keys or our glasses is that putting these objects down is the most ordinary of occurrences, part and parcel of the most humdrum aspects of our lives. (Believe it or not, according to *Readers Digest*, the average adult spends *16 hours a year* trying to find his or her keys.) We have trouble remembering facts and formulas from books and classroom lectures for the same reason. To be schooled is to be bombarded with facts day in and day out. How do you make those facts memorable? (By the way, has anyone seen my glasses?)

Beef up your RAM

In order to understand how to make the important facts memorable, how to keep them stored safely at least until final exams, let's first take a look at how the brain and, more specifically, memory work.

I'm going to call upon a rather useful, and for that reason somewhat overused, analogy, and ask you to think of your brain as that computer you typed your last paper on — an organic computer, wired with nerves, hooked up to various INPUT devices (your five senses), and possessed of both ROM (read-only memory) and RAM (random-access memory).

The ROM is the data you can't touch — the operating system, the information that tells your heart to pump and your lungs to breathe.

On the other hand, RAM is much more accessible. Like most PCs nowadays, your brain stores RAM in two places: *short-term* memory (that old single-sided, low density floppy disk you've been meaning to get rid of) and _long-term_ memory (that one-gigabyte baby on the hard drive).

Okay, so what happens to INPUT in this system?

Let's play memory tag

Given the bombardment of data we receive every day, our brains constantly are making choices. Data either goes in one ear and out the other, or it stops in short-term memory. But when that old floppy disk gets full, the brain is left with a choice—jettison some old information or pass it on to the hard drive.

How does it make a decision _which_ information to pass on and _where_ to store it?

Well, scientists aren't positive about this yet, but, of course, they have theories.

The most readily stored and accessed is data that's been _rehearsed_—gone over again and again. Most of us readily access our knowledge of how to read, how to drive, the year Columbus "discovered" America, the name of the first president of the United States, and other basics without any difficulty at all. (At worst, you remember "Columbus sailed the ocean blue in 1492." And aren't we lucky he did? Otherwise, if only in the interests of historical accuracy, we'd have to remember something like "Leif Eriksson landed at L'Anse aus Meadows, Newfoundland, somewhere between 997 and 1003.") We've worn familiar paths through our memory banks accessing this type of information.

Why, then, can some people recite the names, symbols, and atomic weights of the elements of the periodic table—while they're playing (and winning) Trivial Pursuit—as easily as they can the date of Columbus's dubious achievement?

To return to our computer analogy, this information has gotten "tagged" or "coded" in some way so that it can be easily retrieved by the user. For instance, before storing a file in your computer's long-term RAM, you give it a name, one that will easily conjure what exactly that file is. In other words, you make the file *stand out* in some way from the host of other files you've stored on your disk drive.

For some people, myriad bits of data are almost automatically tagged so that they can be quite easily and handily stored and retrieved. But most of us, if we are to have exceptional memories, must make a special effort.

Can you twist and shout... and remember?

First and foremost, there are three very different kinds of memory—visual, verbal, and kinesthetic, *each* of which can be strong or weak and only the first two of which are associated with your *brain*. (This is, of course, a gross simplification of what we term "memory." Surveys have found more than a hundred different memory tasks in everyday life that can cause people problems, each of which requires a different strategy! Sorry to break it to you, but just because you've learned an easy way to remember a 100-digit number [see Chapter 8] does *not* guarantee that you won't spend days looking for those darned glasses.)

Most people have the easiest time strengthening their *visual* memories, which is why so many memory techniques involve forming "mental pictures."

To strengthen our verbal memories, we use rhymes, songs, letter substitutions, and other mnemonic gimmicks.

Finally, don't underestimate the importance of kinesthetic memory, or what your *body* remembers. Athletes and dancers certainly don't have to be convinced that the muscles, joints, and tendons of their bodies seem to have their own memories. Neither does anyone who's ever remembered a phone number by moving his fingers and "remembering" how it's dialed.

The next time you have to remember a list, any list, say each item out loud and move some part of your body at the same time. A dancer can do the time step and remember her history lecture. A baseball pitcher can associate each movement of his windup with another item in a list he has to memorize. Even random body movements will do. For example, if you have to memorize a list of countries, just associate each one with a specific movement. For Burundi, lift your right index finger while saying it. For Zimbabwe, rotate your neck. Bend a knee for Equador and raise your left hand for San Marino. Kick Latvia in the shins and twirl your hair for Kampuchea. When you have to remember this list of countries, just start moving! It may look a little strange—especially if you make your movements a little too exotic or dramatic in the middle of geography class—but if it works better than anything else for *you*, who cares?

You can also use this new-found memory as a backup to your brain. While you may still memorize key phone numbers, for example, you may also accompany each recitation with the hand movements necessary to actually dial the number. You'll probably find that even if you forget the "mental" tricks you used, your "body memory" will run (or lift or squat or bend or shake) to the rescue!

Once you learn the tricks...

Students, of course, must possess or develop good memories or they risk mediocrity or failure. The mere act of getting by in school means remembering a lot of dates, mathematical and scientific formulas, historical events, characters and plots, sometimes entire poems. (I had a biology teacher who made us memorize the 52 parts of a frog's body. All of which, of course, have been absolutely essential to my subsequent career success. Just kidding.)

Practically, there are two ways of going about this. The most familiar way is rehearsal or repetition. By any name, it is the process of reading or pronouncing something over and over until you've learned it "by heart." (I really didn't want to hold the parts of a frog *too* close to my heart, though.)

But a much easier way—getting back to our computer analogy—is to tag or code things we are trying to remember and to do so with images and words that are either outrageous or very familiar.

For instance, have you ever wondered how, in the days before index cards, ballpoint pens, or TelePrompTers, troubadours memorized song cycles and politicians memorized lengthy speeches? Well, in the case of the great Roman orator Cicero, it was a matter of associating the parts of his speeches with the most familiar objects in his life—the rooms of his home. Perhaps the opening of a speech would be linked to his bed chamber, the next part to his yard. As he progressed through the speech, he would, in essence, mentally take his usual morning stroll passing through the rooms of his home.

This simple method works very well for a relatively short, related list, such as what you need at the grocery store. You can use the rooms in your house, the items in a particular room, even the route you drive to work. Use the landmarks you see every day to remind you of various items you need to buy at the store.

In other cases, more outrageous associations work much better. The more ridiculous or impossible the association, the more memorable it is. Although absent-mindedness is not one of the problems we will try to solve in this book, a common cure for it illustrates my point.

If you frequently have trouble remembering, say, where you put down your pen, get into the habit of conjuring up some startling image *linking* (a key word later on in this book) the pen and the place. For example, as you're putting your pen down on the kitchen table, think about eating peas off a plate with it or of the pen sticking straight up in a pile of mashed potatoes. Even days later, when you think, "Hmm, where did I leave that pen?" the peas and plate (or mashed potatoes) will come to mind, reminding you of the kitchen table.

...the rest is easy

These are the essential principles of memory for which the computer analogy is particularly apt. After all, when dealing with the mind, as with the machine, the GIGO (garbage in, garbage out) rule applies. If you passively allow your brain's process to decide what and how items are stored, you will have a jumbled memory, from which it is difficult to extract even essential bits of knowledge.

On the other hand, if you are selective and careful about assigning useful tags to the items headed for the long-term memory banks, you are on the way to being able to memorize the Manhattan telephone directory!

CHAPTER 2

And Now for a Little Quiz

IMPROVE YOUR MEMORY

KNOW WHAT you're thinking. You bought this book so you could improve your memory and perform better on exams and those darned pop quizzes, and now I turn around and throw some *more* tests your way. I could note that "them's the breaks!"

Or, as one of my high school teachers used to say, I could encourage you to think of tests as your best friends (no, it wasn't the crazy biology teacher I told you about in the last chapter). In this book, and throughout your academic career, tests will give you the measure of how far you've come...and how far you've got to go. Follow the advice in this book and your score on similar tests in the last chapter should be 25 percent higher.

Test 1: numbers

Look at the number directly below this paragraph for no more than 10 seconds. Then cover the page (or, better yet, close the book and put it aside) and write down as much of it—in order—as you can.

674216899411539273

Test 2: words and definitions

Below are 15 obscure words along with their definitions. Study this list for 60 seconds. Then cover it up and take the test directly below the list. Allow yourself no more than 90 seconds to complete the quiz...and no peeking.

dinar	a former gold coin of the Near East
costard	a large, English variety of apple
valgus	bow-legged
omicron	15th letter of the Greek alphabet
malmsey	a sweet wine from Madeira
glabella	the raised area of bone between the eyebrows
estrade	a slightly raised platform in a room or hall
tiffin	a light lunch
lowery	dark, threatening
thistly	troublesome
edentulous	toothless
ghee	clarified butter made from cows' or buffaloes' milk
sinister	left-handed
horripilation	goose bumps
leppy	an unbranded or motherless calf

Have you studied the words diligently? Okay, no cheating now, fill in the blanks:

1. Until they begin teething, babies are ___.
2. Time-sensitive problems can be especially __.
3. The sky grew ___ just before it started to pour.
4. The professor stands on the ___ when giving lectures.
5. A letter of the Greek alphabet is ___.
6. ___ is an ingredient in many recipes for Indian food.
7. An orphaned calf is called a ___.
8. People who aren't very hungry sometimes eat a ___.
9. Getting hit right between the eyes could damage your ___.
10. In elementary school, there are scissors just for kids who are ___.
11. The pie was made with ___ apples.
12. The scary movie gave me ___ all over my body.
13. Someone who's bow-legged is ___.
14. A sweet wine is ___.
15. Coin collectors would be glad to have a ___.

Test 3: names

Take three minutes to memorize the names of the following directors and their films:

Out of Africa/Sydney Pollack

West Side Story/Robert Wise

Lawrence of Arabia/David Lean

Gentleman's Agreement/Elia Kazan

Casablanca/Michael Curtiz

The Grapes of Wrath/John Ford

It Happened One Night/Frank Capra

From Here to Eternity/Fred Zinnemann
Gigi/Vincente Minnelli
Ben-Hur/William Wyler
Gone With the Wind/Victor Fleming
My Fair Lady/George Cukor
The Sting/George Roy Hill
Gandhi/Richard Attenborough

Time's up! Okay, cover the list and fill in as many of the blanks as you can. If you get last names only, that's fine. Take another three minutes to complete the quiz:

1. *My Fair Lady*   _____
2. *Gone With the Wind*   _____
3. William Wyler   _____
4. *Gandhi*   _____
5. *Out of Africa*   _____
6. *From Here to Eternity*   _____
7. *The Grapes of Wrath*   _____
8. Frank Capra   _____
9. *Terms of Endearment*   _____
10. George Roy Hill   _____
11. *West Side Story*   _____
12. Elia Kazan   _____
13. *Lawrence of Arabia*   _____
14. Michael Curtiz   _____
15. *Gigi*   _____

Test 4: dates

Here are the dates of 12 historical events. Take up to three minutes to memorize them, then cover the page and take the quiz below.

1865   Abraham Lincoln is shot and killed by John Wilkes Booth

1920   Women earn the right to vote

1945   The United Nations is established

1961   Alan Shepard becomes the first American in space

1869   The Suez Canal is opened

1796   Edward Jenner discovers a vaccine for smallpox

1852   Harriet Beecher Stowe publishes *Uncle Tom's Cabin*

1989   The Berlin Wall falls

1939   The first jet airplane takes flight

1534   Henry VIII of England breaks with the Catholic Church

1848   The discovery of gold in California marks the beginning of the Gold Rush

1961   Communists build a wall to divide East and West Berlin

🖉🖉🖉

1.   In ____, England's King ____ broke with the Catholic Church.

2.   The Berlin Wall was built in ____ by the ____; it fell in ____.

3.   ____ published *Uncle Tom's Cabin* in ____.

4.   Gold was discovered in ____ in the state of ____.

5.   The United Nations was established in ____.

6.   ____ shot and killed Abraham Lincoln in ____.

7.   The Suez Canal opened in ____.

8.   In ____, the first ____ airplane took flight.

9.   ____ became the first American in space in ____.

10. Edward Jenner discovered a vaccine for ____ in ____.

11. In ____, women earned the right to ____.

Test 5: reading retention

Read the text below, then answer the questions following. Give yourself two minutes to read the text and two minutes to answer the questions *without referring back to the passage*!

The brain is subdivided into four major areas. From the top down, you'll find: 1) the *cerebral cortex,* which I refer to as the cortex; 2) the *midbrain,* which contains a lot of the switching areas where nerves that pass up from below go to and from the cortex; 3) the *brainstem,* where much of the basic nervous system controls sit (coma occurs when this malfunctions, and death occurs when it is severed); and 4) the *cerebellum,* which sits behind the upper part of the brainstem and has traditionally been thought to regulate coordination of complex movements.

The cerebral cortex is the most newly evolved region of the brain and it is the part that separates humans from all the other mammals, especially the area in the front, appropriately named the *frontal cortex.* This area acts as a bridge between the sensory and motor circuits of the rest of the cortex and the older, deeper structures of the limbic system, which regulate drive and emotion. The frontal cortex is probably where much of our complex and abstract thoughts occur. It is probably where we put today in context with yesterday and tomorrow. When the frontal lobe is damaged, we become either more reactive and hypersexual like wild animals (without the step of logic in between to stop us) or very docile and unconcerned.

Behind the frontal cortex are the sensory and motor regions of the cortex, each divided up to correspond with specific areas on the opposite side of the body. Along the side are two protruding horns of cortex called the *temporal lobes*. Here, much of the processing of sound and verbal information occurs. Inside sits a deeper part of the limbic system called the *hippocampus*. The hippocampus acts like a way-station that coordinates the placement of information as it moves from sensory input to other areas of the brain.

In the back is the *occipital cortex*, where much of the processing of visual information occurs. The remaining areas along the side above the temporal horns form the *parietal cortex*. These areas are thought to be where a lot of cross-connection between the different sensory structures occurs. When the right side of the parietal cortex is damaged, very bizarre perceptions and reactions occur, such as ignoring one side of your body because you think it is a stranger.

The limbic system consists of the hippocampus, the rim of cortex on the inside of the halves around the corpus callosum called the *cingulate cortex*, and two almond shaped heads near the frontal region, each one called the *amygdala*. This set of structures is the closest thing to what Freud referred to as the id, the seat of emotion and animal drive. It is the older region of the cortex in terms of evolution, and is also involved in memory.

Strange things can happen when the cortex is damaged. (A great book on this subject is *The Man Who Mistook His Wife for a Hat,* by Dr. Oliver Sacks.) I find this particularly fascinating because it means that who you are as a person in terms of identity and interaction with other people depends completely on the complex and precise interaction of all these neural areas. It suggests that your identity depends on your neurology and not merely on a spirit living in your body.

Questions

1. The most appropriate title for this passage would be ___.

a. The Central Nervous System
b. The Things that Affect the Brain
c. Areas of the Brain
d. The Midbrain

2. The ___ is closely associated with comas and death.

a. brainstem
b. frontal cortex
c. amygdala
d. hippocampus

3. The almond-shaped heads near the frontal region of the limbic system are called the ___.

a. cingulate cortex
b. brainstem
c. hippocampus
d. amygdala

4. The part of the brain that separates humans from other mammals is the ___.

a. cerebral cortex
b. brainstem
c. midbrain
d. cerebellum

5. Processing of sound and verbal information occurs in the ___.

a. occipital cortex
b. temporal lobes
c. cerebellum
d. parietal cortex

Here's another chance to test your memory with some recent history:

Odds are you'll never meet any of the estimated 247 human beings who were born in the past minute. In a population of 6 billion, 247 is a demographic hiccup. In the minute before last, however, there were another 247. In the minutes to come there will be another, then another, then another. By next year at this time, all those minutes will have produced 130 million newcomers to the great human mosh pit. Even after subtracting the deaths each year, the world population is still the equivalent of adding one new Germany.

The last time humanity celebrated a new century there were 1.6 billion people here for the party—or a quarter as many as this time. In 1900 the average life expectancy was, in some places, as low as 23 years; now it's 65, meaning the extra billions are staying around longer and demanding more from the planet.

But things may not be as bleak as they seem. In country after country, birthrates are easing, and the population growth rate is falling.

Cheering as the population reports are becoming today, for much of the past 50 years, demographers were bearers of mostly bad tidings. It was not until the century was nearly two-thirds over that scientists and governments finally bestirred themselves to do something about it. The first great brake on population growth came in the 1960s, with the development of the birth-control pill. In 1969 the United Nations created the U.N. Population Fund, a global organization dedicated to bringing family-planning techniques to women who would not otherwise have them.

Such efforts have paid off in a big way. According to U.N. head counters, the average number of children produced per couple in the developing world—a figure that reached 4.9 earlier this century—has plunged to just 2.7.

But bringing down birthrates loses some of its effectiveness as mortality rates also fall. When people live longer, populations grow not just bigger but also older and frailer.

For now the answer may be to tough things out for a while, waiting for the billions of people born during the great population boom to live out their long lives, while at the same time continuing to reduce birthrates further so that things don't get thrown out of kilter again.

According to three scenarios published by the U.N., the global population in the year 2050 will be somewhere between 7.3 billion and 10.7 billion, depending on how fast the fertility rate falls. The difference between the high scenario and the low scenario? Just one child per couple.

Questions

6. At the world's current growth rate, each year the number of people born is akin to the number of people in ___.

a. China
b. the United States
c. Germany
d. France

7. The average number of children each couple have in the developing world is now ___.

a. 1.6
b. 2.7
c. 4.9
d. 6.3

8. World population is expected to be between 7.3 and 10.7 billion in the year ___.

a. 2010
b. 2025
c. 2050
d. 2100

9. The first major brake on population growth is credited to ___.

a. Germany
b. the fall of world mortality rates
c. the U.N. Population Fund
d. the birth control pill

10. What would be the best title for this passage?

a. Overpopulation: How We Got Here and Where to Go
b. What to Do With an Overpopulated Planet
c. Family-Planning for the New Millennium
d. The Importance of Birthrates

To check how you did in this last test section, see the answers on page 42. Go back and check the book itself to figure out the answers to the others.

How did you do?

Take a piece of paper and write down the scores you got on each of these exercises. This will indicate how much improvement you need to successfully recall the material you learn in school. It will also provide a benchmark so that you can see how far you've come when you take similar quizzes in the last chapter.

The emphasis of these tests was not arbitrary. It corresponds exactly with the skills you will be learning throughout this book: memorizing chains of information (such as the film/director and the date/event pairings), developing a sense for numbers, remembering what you read, and getting a better grasp on vocabulary.

Answers to Test 5:

1. c   6. c
2. a   7. b
3. d   8. c
4. a   9. d
5. b   10. a

CHAPTER 3

Roy G. Biv and Friends

N Chapter 1 we talked about the need to establish tags or codes for items we wish to remember so that our minds will have relatively little difficulty retrieving them from long-term memory.

In this chapter, we will begin talking about one of the methods used for "tagging" items *before they enter* that morass of memory.

The "chain-link" method will help you remember items that appear in sequence, whether it's the association of a date with an event, a scientific term with its meaning, or other facts or objects that are supposed to "go together."

The basis for the chain-link system is that memory works best when you associate the unfamiliar with the familiar, though sometimes the association may be very odd. But to really make it effective, the odder the better.

Our boy Roy

One of the simplest methods is to try to remember just the first letter of a sequence. That's how "Roy G. Biv" (the colors of the spectrum, in order from left to right—red, orange, yellow, green, blue, indigo, violet) got famous. Or "Every Good Boy Does Fine," to remember the notes on a musical staff. Or, perhaps the simplest of all, "FACE," to remember the notes in between. (The latter two work opposite of Roy—using *words* to remember *letters*.) Of course, not many sequences work out as nicely as HOMES, an effective way to remember the Great Lakes (Huron, Ontario, Michigan, Erie, and Superior). If you tried to memorize the signs of the zodiac with this method, you'd wind up with (A)ries, (T)aurus, (G)emini, (C)ancer, (L)eo, (V)irgo, (L)ibra, (S)corpio, (S)agittarius, (C)apricorn, (A)quarius, (P)isces. Now maybe you can make a name or a place or something out of ATGCLVLSSCAP, but I can't!

One solution is to make up a simple sentence that uses the first letters of the list you're trying to remember as the first letters of each word. For example, "**A T**all **G**iraffe **C**hewed **L**eaves **V**ery **L**ow, **S**ome **S**low **C**ows **A**t **P**lay."

Wait a minute! It's the same number of words. Why not just figure out some way to memorize the first set of words? What's better about the second set? A couple of things. First of all, it's easier to picture the giraffe and cow and what they're doing. As we'll soon see, creating such mental images is a very powerful way to remember almost anything. Second, because the words in our sentence bear some relationship to each other, they're much easier to remember. Go ahead, try it. See how long it takes you to memorize the sentence versus all the signs.

Remember: Make your sentence(s) memorable to *you*. *Any* sentence or series of words that helps you remember these letters will do. Here are just two more I created in a few seconds: **A T**all **G**irl **C**alled **L**ively **V**era **L**oved to **S**ip **S**odas from **C**ans **A**nd **P**lates. **A**ny **T**iny **G**erbil **C**ould **L**ove **V**enus. **L**ong **S**illy **S**nakes **C**ould **A**ll **P**ray. Isn't it easy to make up silly, memorable pictures in your head for these?

There is a limit to this technique: Unless the list itself is familiar to you (like the colors of the spectrum), this method will do you little good. For example, medical students for decades have used the mnemonic **O**n **O**ld **O**lympia's **T**owering **T**op **A** **F**inn **A**nd **G**erman **V**ault **A**nd **H**op to remember the list of cranial nerves (olfactory, optic, oculomotor, trochlear, trigeminal, abducens, facial, auditory, glossopharyngeal, vagus, accessory, and hypoglossal). The only way the letter "G" in "German" is going to remind you of "glossopharyngeal" is if you have already spent a significant amount of time studying (memorizing?) this list!

The rain in Spain

Let's say that I was a history major who wanted to remember the year President Nixon resigned, which was 1974.

The usual way for me to do this would be to repeat "Nixon, resignation, 1974, Nixon, resignation, 1974..." *ad nauseum*. How much easier would it be to just say "Nixon walked out the door in '74"! I've established a link between Nixon's resignation (him walking out the door – and out of the presidency) and 1974, the date he resigned. (You'll learn more about how to remember dates in Chapter 8.)

In addition, I was able to use another terrific memory technique – rhyming. Rhyme schemes, no matter how silly or banal, can help us remember things for years. For instance, who can forget that it's "*i* before *e* except after *c*, or when it sounds like *a* as in *neighbor* and *weigh*"?

The stranger the better

Let's step away from schoolwork for a moment to consider the case of a woman who can't remember where she puts anything—car keys, wallet, her month-old baby (just kidding!).

Using the chain-link method would ensure that she would never forget. For instance, let's say she puts her car keys down on her kitchen counter and, as she does, thinks of a car plowing right into the kitchen and through the countertop. Will that woman be able to forget what she did with her keys? Would you?

Or, to pick an example more germane to academic life, let's say that you wanted to remember that *mitosis* is the process whereby one cell divides itself into two. Instead of repeating word and definition countless times, why not think, "My toes is dividing," and form a mental picture of two of your toes separating? Much easier, isn't it?

To make life even easier for those of you forever forgetting your keys, make it a habit to simply put them in the same place every time—in a particular corner of the table, on a hook, wherever—and never, *ever* deviate. It will be one less thing to remember (and, if you believe *Readers Digest*, save you 16 hours a year!).

Flower power

The best way to teach this technique is by example, so let's take another one. Suppose you wanted to remember the following list of nine states and their flowers: New York (Rose), New Jersey (Purple Violet), Texas (Bluebonnet), Maryland (Black-eyed Susan), Minnesota (Lady's Slipper), Oregon (Oregon Grape), Oklahoma (Mistletoe), Tennessee (Iris), and Rhode Island (Violet).

Study the list for no more than two minutes, cover up the page, and try to write down as many combinations as you remember. Heck, you don't even have to do them in order (but you get serious extra credit if you do!).

How did you do? Did you get them all right? How long do you think you'd have to study this list to be able to recite it perfectly? I guarantee you it would take a lot less time if you established a chain link that you could just reel in and out of your memory bank.

Here's how I would remember this list (and remember, make your pictures, associations, and stories memorable to *you*!):

On Sunday mornings, I normally RISE early to play TEN-NIS. But today, I ROSE a little later so we could go to a NEW YORK Yankees' game.

Driving from NEW JERSEY, we saw a brilliant VIOLET ROAD sign that declared: This way to Manhattan ISLAND. (Picture the colorful road sign in your mind.)

At Yankee Stadium, we sat with our friends TEX, MARY (his wife), MINNIE, and SUSAN. TEX's wife was wearing a beautiful new BLUE BONNET. But it was a rough afternoon. First, a LADY'S SLIPPER fell right into MINNIE'S SODA. Then we discovered that all the GRAPES WERE GONE. MARY got so angry that she LANDED a punch and gave SUSAN a BLACK EYE. Luckily, we asked an acquaintance in the next box, MISS LITTLE TOE, if we could have some of her grapes and she said "OK."

Now, this story works for me because I usually *do* play tennis on Sunday mornings. And, as I'm sitting here writing, I actually am planning to skip tennis tomorrow morning in order to attend a Yankee game. So all of these images are perfectly natural and memorable *to me*. Just as your story needs to be memorable *to you*.

Is this efficient?

You're probably wondering just how much time it took me to construct these ridiculous associations and the story to go with them. The answer: about three minutes. I'll bet it will take you a lot longer to memorize the list of states and flowers. And my way of doing this is so much more fun! Not only that, but I'd be willing to bet that you'll remember "Mary landed a punch and gave Susan a black eye" a lot longer than "Maryland" and "Black-eyed Susan."

The reason is that you use so much more of your brain when you employ techniques like this. Reciting a list of facts over and over to yourself uses only three of your faculties — sight (as you read them from the page), speech, and hearing — in carving the memory trail. Constructing a visual story like the one we just did also puts to work your imagination, perhaps the most powerful of your mind's many powers.

Those were the days...

Let's try another example, one with which I doubt most of you are at all familiar — the months of the Islamic calendar: Mohorran, Safar, Rabi I, Rabi II, Jumada I, Jumada II, Rajab, Shaban, Ramadan, Shawwal, Dhu 'l-Qada, and Dhu 'l-hijjah.

Here's the way I would remember these months:

I'm in the desert, on a *safari*, with *two rabbis,* Joe and Ben. (Whew! Three months in one sentence!) We decide to stop and eat. I held up *two* big sandwiches and tried to *show* them to *Ben*, but he got *mad* that *Joe* hadn't used enough meat. "*More ham*" he cried, which was a very strange thing for a rabbi to yell. Before I knew it, Joe had thrown a *right jab* right at Ben. Luckily, we noticed a *Ramada* Inn right up ahead, with a huge, blue genie wearing a *shawl* standing in front of it. But Ben was still mad. "Joe, I challenge you to a *duel*, you *cad*." "Oh, yeah," cried Joe, as he *hitched up* his robes. "Well, I challenge you to a *duel, too*."

Remember, it's not enough to memorize this kind of story and use the words as triggers for your memory. You must create the picture in your mind — the two rabbis on camels, the sandwich that needs more ham, the right jab thrown by Joe, the Ramada Inn in the middle of the desert with a genie in front. Make each of them stand out in your mind. Perhaps the genie looks like your grandmother, what with the shawl and all. Perhaps the ham is green (presuming you're a Dr. Seuss fan). Whatever it takes to make *your* pictures easily recallable and memorable.

Now you try. How would you remember another obscure list, such as this longer one of cat breeds? Abyssinian, American Brown, American Shorthair, Bombay, Birman, Burmese, Colorpoint Shorthair, Cornish Rex, Devon Rex, Egyptian Mau, Exotic, Havana Brown, Korat, Maine Coon, Manx, Ocicat, Oriental, Persian, Ragdoll, Russian Blue, Scottish Fold, Siamese, Somali, Tonkinese, Turkish Angola.

Time yourself. When you can construct a series of pictures to remember a list like this — and remember it for a while, not just a day — all in less than five minutes, you are well on your way to mastering this powerful memory technique.

Hear my song

Observations of people who have been in accidents or suffered other types of severe brain trauma have yielded many interesting insights into the ways our minds and memories work. For instance, people who have had the left side of their brains damaged might lose their ability to speak and remember words and facts, but often are still able to sing songs perfectly.

Current thinking on this is that the faculty for speech resides in the left hemisphere of the brain, while the ability to sing can be found in the right.

It is my feeling that the more of your mind's power you put behind the job of remembering, the better you'll do, so I'd like to suggest song as another great way to remember strings of information.

For instance, I remember few things from chemistry class in my junior year of high school (not having had memory training at that time). But one thing I'll never forget is that ionization is a dissociative reaction; it is the result of electrons becoming separated from their nuclei.

The reason I remember this is that Mr. Scott, my chemistry teacher, came into class singing (to the main theme from the opera "Grenada") "I-, I-, I-onization. I-, I-, I-onization. Oh, this is, oh, this is a dissociative reaction in chemistry."

Or there's the case of one of Robert Frost's most loved poems, "Stopping by Woods On a Snowy Evening." Did you ever realize that you could sing the entire poem to the music of "Hernando's Hideaway" by Xavier Cugat?

Try it with the last four lines—"The woods are lovely dark and deep, but I have promises to keep, and miles to go before I sleep. And miles to go before I sleep." Trust me: it works for the whole poem. Unfortunately, that beautiful poem, one of my favorites, may now be ruined forever!

Just do it

Music is one of the ways that you can create a chain link to improve your memory. As the examples we've already discussed show, there are many others:

Unusual. To the extent possible, make the chain-link scenarios you construct highly unusual.

Active. Don't think of an object just sitting there. Have it do something! Remember Mom and her car smashing through the kitchen counter earlier in the chapter? How can such an image be forgotten?

Emotional. Conjure up a scenario in establishing your chain link that elicits an emotional reaction—joy, sorrow, physical pain, whatever.

Rhyming. Many lessons for preschoolers and those just in first and second grades are done with rhymes. If it works for them, it should work for you, right?

Acronyms. If you've taken trigonometry, you've probably come across good old Chief *SOH-CAH-TOA*. If you've been lucky enough to evade trig (or didn't have Mr. Oldehoff in 11th grade), you've missed one of the easiest ways to remember trigonometric functions: *S*ine equals *O*pposite/ *H*ypotenuse; *C*osine equals *A*djacent/*H*ypotenuse; *T*angent equals *O*pposite/*A*djacent.

Relax and have fun

You're probably thinking that all of this doesn't sound like it will make your life any easier. I know it *seems* like a lot of work to think of soundalikes, associations, and pictures and construct crazy scenarios or songs using them. Trust me: If you start applying these tips *routinely*, they will quickly become second nature and make you a more efficient student.

There's the rub

The only problem with this method is that you might occasionally have trouble remembering what your soundalike signified in the first place. But the process of forming the link will, more often than not, obviate the problem because the link to the original item is made stronger by the act of forming these crazy associations. Again, the crazier they are, the more *memorable* they are.

In the next chapter, we'll get away from straight factual memory for a little while and talk about how we can get a better grasp of material as we read through it the first time.

CHAPTER 4

Reading and Remembering

OTHING YOU DO as you pursue your studies *in any subject* will serve you as well as learning to read — and remembering what you've read, whenever you need to. The ability to recall a great amount of detail *without* having to review is a tremendous benefit to *any* student.

In college, where the reading demands of a *single* course can be voluminous, just think how much more students could get out of texts and how much more efficiently they could prepare for exams and term papers if they could get most of the information they need *the first time around!*

This chapter will show you how to do it...easily.

Reading to remember

The best way to begin any reading assignment is to skim the pages to get an overall view of what information is included in the text. Then, read the text in detail and highlight it and/or take notes in your notebook.

I'm going to digress for a moment, taking your side, to criticize a large number, perhaps even the majority, of the texts you're forced to plow through. This criticism is constructive: I want to show you the deficiencies in textbooks that you will have to overcome in order to be the best student you can be *without unnecessary effort*.

Think of the differences in writing and presentation between newspapers and textbooks. Newspapers are edited and designed to make reading simple. Most newspaper articles are organized using the "pyramid" approach: The first paragraph (the top of the pyramid) makes the major point of the story, then successive paragraphs add more detail and make related points, filling out the pyramid. You can get a pretty good handle on the day's news by reading the headlines and the first few paragraphs of each story. If you're interested in more details, just read on.

Textbooks, on the other hand, usually are *not* written to allow for such an approach. Many times authors begin with a relatively general introduction to the material, and then lead readers through their reasoning to major points.

The next time you have to read a history, geography, or similar text, try skimming the assigned pages first. Read the heads, subheads, and callouts, those brief notes or headings in the outside margins of each page that summarize the topic covered in the section. Read the first sentence of each paragraph. Then go back and read the details.

To summarize the skimming process:

1. Read and be sure you understand the title or heading. Try rephrasing it as a question for further clarification of what you read.

2. Examine all the subheadings, illustrations, and graphics — these will all help you identify the significant matter within the text.

3. Read thoroughly the introductory paragraphs, the chapter summary, and any questions at the chapter's end.

4. Read the first sentence of every paragraph — this generally includes the main idea.

5. Evaluate what you have gained from this process: Can you answer the questions at the end of the chapter? Could you intelligently participate in a class discussion of the material?

6. Write a brief summary that capsulizes what you have learned from your skimming.

7. Based on this evaluation, decide whether a more thorough reading is required.

I've found that the most effective way to read a textbook is to first go through reading the headlines, subheadings, and the callouts so that I know the major points of the chapter *before* I get to them. Then I'm more attuned to absorb when I arrive at these sections. In other words, by the time I get to the material for which I am reading the chapter, my antennae are up and my mind is ready to soak everything up.

What if, despite your best efforts and my best advice, you simply cannot slog through another chapter? You simply can't fathom what the author is talking about? *It may not be your fault.* You will undoubtedly be assigned at least one textbook during your school life that is so obtuse you aren't sure whether to read it front to back, upside down, or inside out.

Don't keep wasting your time. Go to the library or bookstore and find another book that covers the same subject area, one that you *can* understand. (Your teacher or professor may even be able to recommend an alternative text —

unless, of course, he or she wrote the unintelligible one, something that's not uncommon at the college level.) As long as both books cover relatively the same ground, you will save yourself a lot of time, energy, and frustration by substituting one for the other.

Reading faster without speed reading

While the heads, subheads, first sentences, and other author-provided hints will help you get a quick read on what a chapter's about, some of the *words* in that chapter will help you concentrate on the important points and ignore the unimportant. Knowing when to speed up, slow down, ignore, or really concentrate will help you read both faster *and* more effectively.

When you see words like "likewise," "moreover," "also," "furthermore," and the like, you should know nothing new is being introduced. If you already know what's going on, speed up or skip what's coming entirely.

On the other hand, when you see words like "on the other hand," "nevertheless," "however," "rather," "but," and their ilk, it's time to slow down—you're getting information that certainly adds a new perspective—it may even contradict what you've just read.

Watch out for "payoff" words such as, "in conclusion," "therefore," "thus," "consequently," "to summarize"—especially if you only have time to "hit the high points" of a chapter or if you're reviewing for a test. Here's where the real meat is, where everything that went before is happily tied up in a nice fat bow, a present that enables you to avoid having to unwrap the entire chapter.

One chapter at a time

Sometimes students have a desire to rush through the reading of textbooks to "get it over with." Granted, there are textbook writers who seem to go out of their way to encourage such a reaction. Don't fall into the trap.

Instead, before getting to the next chapter as rapidly as possible, stop to perform the following exercise:

- ✎ Write down definitions of any key terms you think are essential to *understanding* the topic.

- ✎ Write down questions and answers that you think help *clarify* the topic. Play teacher for a minute and design a pop quiz on the chapter.

- ✎ Write questions for which you *don't have the answers*, then go back and find them by rereading the chapter, noting questions you'd like to ask the professor or answer through further reading.

When reading is a formula

Texts for mathematics, economics, and science require a slightly different treatment. You should follow the steps just outlined, but with one important addition: Make sure that you thoroughly understand the concepts expressed in the various charts and graphs and do *not* move on to the next section unless you have mastered the previous one.

You must understand one section before moving on to the next, because the next concept is usually *based* on the previous one. If there are sample problems, solve those that tie in with the section you have just read to make sure that you understand the concepts imparted. If you still fail to grasp a key concept or equation, start again and try again. But *don't* move on — you'll just be wasting your time.

These texts require such a slow, steady approach, even one with a lot of backtracking or, for that matter, a lot of wrong turns. "Trial and error" *is* an accepted method of scientific research. The key, though, is to make it *informed* trial and error — having a clear idea of where you're heading and *learning* from each error. While trial and error is okay, it is much more important to be able to easily apply the same analysis (solution, reasoning) to a slightly different problem, which requires real understanding. Getting the right answer just because you eliminated every *wrong* one may be a very viable strategy for taking a test, but it's a lousy way to assure yourself you've actually learned something.

Understanding is especially essential in any technical subject. It's easy for some of you to do well on math tests because you have a great memory, are lucky, or have an innate math "sense." Trust me, sooner or later your luck runs out, your memory overloads, and your calculations stop making sense. You *will* reach a point where, without understanding, you will be left confused on the shore, watching your colleagues sail heroically to the promised land.

Whether math and science come easily to you or make you want to find the nearest pencil-pocketed computer nerd and throttle him, there are some ways you can do better at such technical subjects, without the world's greatest memory, a lot of luck or any "radar":

- ✎ Whenever you are able, "translate" formulas and numbers into words. To test your understanding, try to put your translation into *different* words.

- ✎ Even if you're not a particularly visual person, pictures can often help. Try translating a particularly vexing math problem into a drawing or diagram.

- ✎ Before you even get down to solving a problem, is there any way for you to estimate the answer or, at least the range within which the answer should fall (greater than one, but less than 10)? This is the easy way to make sure you wind up in the right ballpark.

- ✎ Play around. There are often different paths to the same solution or even equally valid solutions.

If you find one, try to find others. This is a great way to increase your understanding of all the principles involved.

✎ When you are checking your calculations, try working backwards. I've found it an easier way to catch simple mathematical errors.

✎ Try to figure out what is being asked, what principles are involved, what information is important, what's not.

I can't resist an example here: A 33 1/3 rpm record is 6.57 inches in diameter. The label is two inches wide. The song lasts for exactly three minutes, 14 seconds. The record is .012 inches thick. Here's the question: How many grooves does the record have?

✎ Teach someone else. Trying to explain mathematical concepts to someone else will quickly pinpoint what you really know or don't know. It's virtually impossible to get someone *else* — especially someone who is slower than you at all this stuff — to understand the material if *you* don't.

By the way, the answer to the question about the grooves in the record is one. If the record didn't have one continuous groove, the music wouldn't keep playing! In case you didn't notice, *none* of the mathematical information provided had the slightest bearing on the answer.

You should approach foreign language texts the same way, especially basic texts that teach vocabulary (we'll deal with memorizing vocabulary words in the next chapter) and fundamental rules of grammar. If you haven't mastered the words you're supposed to in the first section, you'll have trouble reading the story at the end of the third.

Follow the yellow brick road

When I discovered highlighters during my first year of college, my reaction was, "Where have you been all my life?" I couldn't believe how terrific they were for zeroing in on the really important material in a text. However, I soon realized that I was highlighting *too much* – rereading highlighted sections became nearly the same as reading the whole darn text again.

I developed this set of rules for making the most of my highlighters during college, when my workload became much heavier:

1. I highlighted areas of the text with which I didn't feel completely comfortable.

2. I identified single words and sentences that encapsulated a section's major ideas and themes.

3. I underlined to make studying easier. I concentrated on the key words, facts, and concepts, and skipped the digressions, multiple examples, and unnecessary explanations.

4. I underlined my classroom notes as well as texts to make studying from *them* easier.

To sharpen your underlining skills, read through the next three paragraphs and indicate with your highlighter the key sentence(s) or words:

When told to communicate, most people immediately think of writing or speaking. Yet, there is another form of communication that everyone uses — without realizing it. Through various facial expressions, body movements and gestures, we all have a system of nonverbal communication.

We constantly signal to others our feelings and attitudes unconsciously through actions we may not even realize we are performing. One type is called barrier signals. Because most people usually feel safer behind a barrier, they often unthinkingly fold their arms or find some other pretext for placing their arms in front of their body when they feel insecure.

Such nonverbal communication can lead to serious misunderstanding if you are not careful. Take the simple symbol you make by forming a circle with your thumb and forefinger. In America it means "Okay." In France, however, it signifies a zero, something — or someone — worthless. Imagine the offense a French waiter might take if you signified your satisfaction with your meal with this sign! You would offend and insult when you intended to praise.

Which of these words or phrases would you underline? I'd probably underline "nonverbal communication," "barrier signals," and "insecure" (with an arrow drawn to "barrier signals" to remind me of the reason they're used) in the first paragraph.

And I would probably underline the first sentence in the second paragraph, which summarizes the point of the article.

Do you think you would underline anything in the third paragraph? Why wouldn't you? It's an example — a nice one, a simple one, an understandable one — but if you understand the concept, you really don't need anything else.

If you had to review the text for an exam, you would glance at the one sentence and four or five words you highlighted to get the gist of the three paragraphs. This would save you a tremendous amount of time.

Retention

The word "retention" is frequently mentioned alongside reading.

Retention is the process by which we keep imprints of past experiences in our minds, the "storage depot." Subject to other actions of the mind, what is retained can be recalled when needed. Items are retained in the same order in which they are learned. So, your studying should build one fact, one idea, one concept on another.

Broad concepts can be retained much more easily than details. Master the generalities and the details will fall into place.

If you think something is important, you will retain it more easily. An attitude that says, "I *will* retain this," *will* help you remember. So, convincing yourself that what you are studying is something you *must* retain and recall *increases* your chance of adding it to your long-term memory bank.

As I mentioned in the last chapter, let yourself react to the data you are reading. Associating new information with what you already know will make it easier to recall.

Still having trouble?

If you follow these suggestions and are still having trouble retaining what you read, try these other ideas. They are a bit more time-consuming, but undoubtedly will help you.

Take notes

Do you own the book you're reading? Do you not care about preserving it for posterity? Then use its margins for notes. Go beyond mere highlighting to assign some ranking to the facts conveyed by the text.

I used to use a little shorthand method to help me remember written materials. I'd draw vertical lines close to the text to assign levels of importance. One vertical line meant that the material should be reviewed; two indicated that the facts were very important; asterisks would signify "learn or fail" material. I'd insert question marks for material that I wanted one of my more intelligent friends or the teacher to explain to me further. I'd use circles to indicate the information I was dead sure would show up on the next test.

Interestingly, I found that the very act of assigning relative weights of importance to the text and keeping a lookout for test material helped me remember because it heightened my attention. (For a more detailed method of taking notes, see Chapter 6.)

Become an active reader

Earlier in this chapter, I urged you to quiz yourself on written material to ascertain how well you'd retained it. If this doesn't work, try asking the questions _before_ you read the material.

For instance, even though I have been an avid reader throughout much of my academic life, I had some trouble with the reading comprehension sections of standardized tests the first couple of times I attempted them. Why? I think I had a tendency to rush through these sections.

Then someone suggested to me that I read the questions _before_ I read the passage. Presto! Great scores in reading comp (765 points on my verbal SAT for all of you doubters!).

While you won't always have such a ready-made list of questions, there are other sources—the summaries at the beginnings of chapters, the synopses in tables of contents. Pay attention to these.

For instance, if an author states in an introductory paragraph, "Containing the Unsatisfactory Result of Oliver's Adventure; and a Conversation of Some Importance between Harry Maylie and Rose," as Charles Dickens does in _Oliver Twist_, you may ask yourself:

✎ What was Oliver's unsatisfactory adventure?

✎ What could the result of it have been?

✎ What could Harry and Rose be talking about that's so important?

Believe it or not, this technique will train your mind to hone in on those important details when they arise in the story. It would also be a good idea to ask yourself these questions immediately after you finish the chapter. It will help you ascertain whether you "got" the important points of the chapter and help you retain the information longer.

Understand, don't memorize

Approach any text with the intent of *understanding* it rather than memorizing it. Understanding is a key part of memorization. Don't stop the flow of information during your reading (other than to underline and take notes). Go back and memorize later.

Organize the material

Our minds crave order. Optical illusions work because the mind is bent on imposing order on every piece of information coming in from the senses. As you read, think of ways to organize the material to help your mind absorb it.

I always liked diagrams with single words and short phrases connected with arrows to show cause and effect relationships. Or I would highlight in texts the *reasons* things occurred with a special mark (I used a triangle).

Develop good reading habits

It's impossible for anyone to remember what he read at 3 a.m., or while waiting to go on the biggest date of his life. Set aside quiet time when you're at your best. Are you a morning person? Then wake up early to do your reading. Do you get going at 6 p.m.? Then get your reading done before stopping by the Rathskeller.

Don't forget to use your dictionary to look up terms you don't understand. (Or put the information in the next chapter to use. Then you won't need a dictionary!)

In case you forgot

Each time you attempt to read something that you must recall, use this six-step process to assure you'll remember:

1. **Evaluate the material.** Define your purpose for reading. Identify your interest level and get a sense of how difficult the material is.

2. **Choose appropriate reading techniques** for the purpose of your reading. If you are reading to grasp the main idea, then that is exactly what you will recall.

3. **Identify the important facts** and remember what you need to. Let your purpose for reading dictate what you remember, and identify associations that connect the details to recall.

4. **Take notes.** Use your own words to give a synopsis of the main ideas. Use an outline, diagram, or concept tree to show relationship or pattern. Your notes serve as an important backup to your memory. Writing down key points will further reinforce your ability to remember.

5. **Review.** Quiz yourself on those things you *must* remember. Develop some system by which you review notes at least three times before you are required to recall. The first review should be shortly after you have read, the second should come a few days later, and the final review should take place just before you are expected to recall. This process will help you avoid cram sessions.

6. **Implement.** Find opportunities to *use* the knowledge you have gained. Study groups and class discussions are invaluable opportunities to put what you have learned to good use. Participate in group discussions — they'll greatly increase what you recall.

If you find after all this work that you need still *more* help with reading, comprehension, and recall, I recommend *Improve Your Reading,* one of the other volumes in my *How to Study Program.*

CHAPTER 5

One Chapter
to a Better Vocabulary

THE WAY TO a great vocabulary is at your fingertips, and it has absolutely nothing to do with those word-a-day calendars.

In this chapter, I will show you two ways to improve your memory for sesquipedalian (having many syllables) and small, obscure words.

The building blocks method

Whenever possible, try to remember *concepts* rather than memorizing random data. For instance, if someone told you to memorize a long string of numbers—for example, 147101316192225—it would be far better to note that each

The roots of language

Here are two dozen or so roots from Latin and Greek that contribute to thousands of English words:

Root	Meaning	Example
annu	year	annual
aqua	water	aquarium
arch	chief	archenemy
bio	life	biology
cap, capt	take, seize	capture
chron	time	chronological
dic, dict	say	indicate
duc, duct	lead	induction
fact, fect	do, make	effective
fer	carry, bear	infer
graph	write	graphics
homo	same, identical	homonym
logos	word	logical
manu	hand	manufacture
mitt, miss	send	remittance
path	feel, feeling	apathy
ped, pod	foot	pedal
plico	fold	implication
pon, posit	place, put	imposition
port	carry	export
psyche	mind	psychopathic
scrib	write	scribe
spec	observe, see	speculative
tend, tent	stretch	intention
tene,	have, hold	tenacious
vert, vers	turn	introverted

number is three higher than the one before (1, 4, 7, 10, 13, and so on) and simply remember that rule.

Similarly, it is far better to absorb the way words are constructed, to memorize a relatively small number of prefixes, suffixes, and roots, rather than trying to cram the contents of _Webster's Dictionary_ into your already crowded memory.

A note on English

Our borrowed mother tongue, English, is perhaps the most democratic of all languages. Built on a Celtic base, it has freely admitted a multitude of words from other languages, particularly French, Latin, Greek, German, and a rich body of slang (from anywhere we could get it).

The oldest branches in this diverse family tree, Celtic and Old English, are the least amenable to some of the techniques we are about to learn. These are basically simple words, not built in complicated fashion as are Latinate and Greek terms.

However, as anyone addicted to crossword puzzles can tell you, our language is replete with myriad Romance words (those from French, Italian, and Spanish) that often can be dissected into rather simple elements.

The cart before the horse

As the list of root words suggests, knowing its definition alone is usually not enough. Prefixes, the fragments added to the beginning of a word, can greatly change the message conveyed by the root. Here are some examples of common prefixes:

Prefix	Meaning	Example
a-, ab-	from, away	aberration
a-, an-	without, not	amoral
ad-, af-, at-, ag-	to, toward	admonition
		affection
		aggressor
ant-, anti-	against	antidote
ante-	before	antecedent
bi-	two	bicycle
con-, com-	with, together	commitment
de-	away from	deviant
dis-	apart, opposite	disrespect
e-, ex-	out of, over	exorbitant
en-	in	envelope
extra-	beyond	extraordinary
hyper-	above, over	hyperthermia
hypo-	under	hypoglycemic
il-, im-, in-	not	illicit
		impeccable
inter-	between	intercept
intra-	within	intrauterine
mal-	evil	maladjusted
multi-	many	multiply
ob-, op-	toward, against	obdurate
		opposite
per-	through	perspicacious
peri-	around	peripatetic
post-	after	posthumous
pre-	before	premonition

Prefix	Meaning	Example
pro-	for, forth	production
re-	again, back	regression
sub-, sup-	under	substantiate
sym-, syn-	with, together	sympathetic synergy
tri-	three	triangle
un-	not	uncool

The tail that wags the dog

The last, but certainly not the least important building block of words is the suffix, which quite often indicates how the word is being used. Suffixes can be used to turn an adjective into an adverb (the "-ly" ending), to compare things (smallER, smallEST), or even to modify other suffixes (liveLIEST). Some suffixes with which you should be familiar are:

Suffix	Meaning	Example
-able, -ible	capable of	pliable
-ac, -al, -ial	pertaining to	hypochondriac remedial
-acy	quality of	fallacy, legacy
-age	quality of	outage
-ance, -ence	state of being	abundance
-ant, -ent	one who	student
-ary	devoted to	secretary
-cy	state of	lunacy
-dom	quality of, state of	martyrdom kingdom

Suffix	Meaning	Example
-en	made of	wooden
-er, -or	one who	perpetrator
-ful	full of	woeful
-hood	state of	neighborhood
-ic	pertaining to	pedantic
-ine	like	leonine
-ion	act of	extermination
-ish, -ity	quality of	purplish, enmity
-ist	one who practices	novelist
-ive	disposition of	active
-less	lacking	penniless
-ly	like	cowardly
-ment	process of	enlightenment
-ness	state of	holiness
-ory	pertaining to	memory
-ose	full of	grandiose
-ous	like	porous
-ry	state of	ribaldry
-some	full of	toothsome

Practice those prefixes and suffixes

Of course, I don't expect that you'll memorize these lists. But if you read them over a few times, paying particular attention to the examples, you'll absorb the roots, prefixes, and suffixes fairly quickly.

Here's a list of 20 words. Write the definition in the blank space using what you remember of the building blocks of words above. Then, check to see how you did using the lists above.

1. Antiquated   _____
2. Preapproval   _____
3. Hyperthyroidism   _____
4. Noncontrollable   _____
5. Horrific   _____
6. Oncologist   _____
7. Chivalry   _____
8. Combustion   _____
9. Intermittent   _____
10. Transcendant   _____
11. Sensory   _____
12. Periodic   _____
13. Intercranial   _____
14. Postsurgical   _____
15. Obstruction   _____
16. Neonatology   _____
17. Hydrophobic   _____
18. Devotional   _____
19. Visionary   _____
20. Misdefined   _____

Method with madness in it

How did you do on the quiz? I'll bet a lot better than you thought, simply because of this rather brief introduction to etymology.

Now let's examine another way of remembering so that you can have powerful words at your disposal — the soundalike method. As we saw in Chapter 3, forming your own associations — sometimes wildly outrageous ones — can be quite helpful in carving easy-access roads to the long-term memory banks.

In order to use this method, create a scenario using the soundalike of the word or parts of the word and the definition of the word.

Consider this example: Let's say that you've seen the word "ostracize" countless times, but can never quite remember that it means "to cast out from a group." You could then create this nonsense thought: "The ostrich's eyes are so big, no one wants to look at him."

In such an example, you would be using the size of the ostrich and creating an absurd reason he might be a cast out. Or, I could have made the phrase: "The ostrich's size was so big he was thrown out of his hole."

Sure, you're saying, that's an easy example. But let's take another one. Since we're in a chapter on vocabulary, let's consider "sesquipedalian," which means "having many syllables" or "tending to use long words." Our soundalike association could be: "She says quit peddling those big words."

Or, one picture might be worthy of a particular vocabulary word. You might associate the difficult-to-remember word not with a phrase, but with an outrageous picture.

For instance, to remember that the word "flambe" means a food covered with flames, think of a plate of food with bees whose wings are ablaze flying from it.

Again, as we learned in Chapter 3, this sort of exercise is not a lot of work, but it is a great deal of fun. It'll help your mind hold onto words, even those you use infrequently, forever.

Here's a list of "50-cent words" with soundalikes that will make them easy to learn:

Cutaneous (pertaining to or affecting the skin): "Cute skin, ain't it just?"

Necromancy (a method of divination through invocation of the dead): "Nancy, dig up Phil Niekro."

Hoosegow (slang for a jail): "Who's cow is in jail?"

Welter (to toss or heave): "Toss it here, Walter!"

Sullage (sewage or waste): "Sully, age is a waste."

Hieromonk (an Eastern monk who was also a priest): "Need a priest? Hire a monk."

Avouch (to declare or assert): " 'Ouch!' he vowed."

Cognomen (a nickname or epithet): "No man was named Cog."

Dikdik (a tiny antelope): "Did did you you see see that that antelope antelope?"

Guayabera (a kind of Cuban sport skirt or jacket): "Put on your shirt and buy me a beer, Fidel."

Liatigo (strap on a Western saddle): "Let that strap go, horsey!"

Petiole (the stalk by which a leaf is attached to a stem): "Pet my old leaf?"

Mizzle (to rain in fine drops): "It's drizzling, Ma."

Jaguarundi (a tropical American wildcat): "Help! There's Jaguar undies on top!"

Frutescent (shrubby): "Smelly fruits grew on the shrub."

Refrangible (capable of being refracted, like rays of light): "Hey, Ray, ball the light for Angie."

Osteophyte (an abnormal outgrowth of bone): "Two bones were fighting, Ossie."

Icosahedron (a solid having 20 faces): "I guess he'd run 20."

Euclase (rare green or blue mineral): "That green gem you got sure is classy."

With this tool, you can become a horribly pedantic conversationalist and never have to run to the dictionary while you're reading _Finnegan's Wake_.

Feel free to use _any_ of the memory methods in this book to remember _any_thing. If you have to remember the word "surreptitious," for example, why not combine the soundalike and chain link methods by picturing a burglar, black mask and all, carrying a bottle of pancake syrup?

Try a sample

Still another method that works quite well—and is relatively easy to employ for some words—is to associate a word with a very particular example. If you're reading an English grammar textbook and you come across the term "oxymoron," which is defined as "a figure of speech combining seemingly contradictory words or phrases," think how much easier it would be to remember if your notes looked like this:

Oxymoron	military intelligence, cruel kindness
Onomatopoeia	PLOP, PLOP, FIZZ, FIZZ
Metaphor	food for thought
Simile	this is *like* that

CHAPTER 6

Taking Notes
to Remember Texts

 HAVE A confession to make, a rather difficult one for someone whose specialty is careers and education: To this very day, I resent having to write an outline for a book, article, or research project. I'd much rather just sit down and start writing.

I would have hated myself in school if I knew then what I know now: You should do outlines while you are *reading,* as well. The fact is, outlines will help you review a text more quickly and remember it more clearly.

In Chapter 4, I advised using highlighters to, well, highlight important messages. This is great in a relatively easy-to-remember text. For other courses, it would be a sure sign of masochism, as it assures only one thing: You will have to read a great deal of your deadly textbooks all over again when exam time rolls around.

Likewise, marginalia usually make the most sense only in context, so the messy method of writing small notes in white space around the text will engender a great deal of rereading as well.

So then, what's *the* most effective way to read and remember your textbooks? *Sigh.* Yes, that good old outline.

Reverse engineering

Outlining a textbook, article, or other secondary source is a little bit like "reverse engineering" — a way of developing a schematic for something so that you can see exactly how it's been put together. Seeing that logic of construction will help you a great deal in remembering the book — by putting the author's points down in *your* words, you will be building a way to retrieve the key points of the book more easily from your memory.

Outlining will force you to distinguish the most important points from those of secondary importance, helping you build a true understanding of the topic.

The bare bones of outlining

Standard outlines use Roman numerals, (I, II, III), capital letters, Arabic numerals (1, 2, 3, 4), and lower-case letters and indentations to show the relationships between and importance of topics in the text. While you certainly don't have to use the Roman-numeral system, your outline would be organized in the following manner:

Title

Author

I. First important topic in the text

    A. First subtopic

        1. First subtopic of A

            a. First subtopic of 1

            b. Second subtopic of 1

        2. Second subtopic of A

II. The second important topic in the text

Get the idea? In a book, the Roman numerals usually would refer to chapters, the capital letters to subheadings, and the Arabic numbers and lower-case letters to blocks of paragraphs. In an article or single chapter, the Roman numerals would correspond to subheadings, capital letters to blocks of paragraphs, Arabic numbers to paragraphs, small letters to key sentences.

What's he getting at?

We understand things in outline form. Ask an intelligent person to recount something and he'll state the main points and only enough details to make his words interesting and understandable. The discipline of creating outlines will help you zero in on the most important points an author is making and capture them, process them, and, thereby, retain them.

Sometimes an author will have the major point of a paragraph in the first sentence. But just as often, the main idea of a paragraph or section will follow some of these telltale words: "therefore," "because," "thus," "since," "as a result."

When you see any of these words, you should identify the material they introduce as the major points in your outline. Material immediately preceding and following almost always will be in support of these major points.

Create a timeline

I always found it frustrating to read textbooks in social studies. I'd go through chapters on France, England, the Far East and have a fairly good understanding of those areas, but have no idea where certain events stood in a global context. As more and more colleges add multicultural curricula, you may find it even more difficult to "connect" events in 17th-century France or 19th-century Africa with what was happening in the rest of the world (let alone the U.S.).

An excellent tool for overcoming that difficulty is a timeline that you can update periodically. It will help you visualize the chronology and remember the relationship of key world events.

For instance, a simple, abridged timeline of James Joyce's literary life would look like this (I would suggest you create a horizontal time line, but the layout of this book makes reproducing it that way difficult. So here's a vertical version.):

1882	Birth
1907	*Chamber Music*
1914	*Dubliners*
1916	*A Portrait of the Artist as a Young Man*
1918	*Exiles*
1922	*Ulysses*
1927	*Pomes Pennyeach*
1937	*Collected Poems*
1939	*Finnegan's Wake*
1941	Death

This makes it easy to see that Joyce was born as the U.S. experienced a post-Civil War boom in industry and population growth and died during World War II. If you added other literary figures from the same period, you would not soon forget that Joyce, Virginia Woolf, Ezra Pound, W.B.

Yeats, Lady Augusta Gregory, Charles Darwin, George Eliot, and D.H. Lawrence, among many others, were all literary contemporaries. Adding nonliterary events to your timeline would enable you to make connections between what was being written and what was going on in the United States, Britain, Europe, Africa, and so forth.

Draw a concept tree

Another terrific device for limiting the amount of verbiage in your notes and making them more memorable is the concept tree. Like a timeline, the concept tree is a visual representation of the relationship among several key facts. For instance, one might depict categories and specific types of animals in this way:

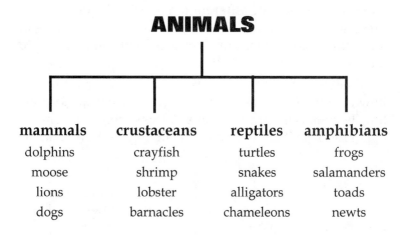

ANIMALS

mammals	**crustaceans**	**reptiles**	**amphibians**
dolphins	crayfish	turtles	frogs
moose	shrimp	snakes	salamanders
lions	lobster	alligators	toads
dogs	barnacles	chameleons	newts

Such devices certainly give further credence to the old saying, "A picture is worth a thousand words," because timelines and concept trees will be much more helpful than mere words in remembering material, particularly conceptual material. Developing them will ensure that your interest in the text will not flag too much.

But don't limit yourself to just these two types of "pictures." Consider using a chart, graph, diagram, or anything else you can think of to reorganize *any* information for *any* class you're taking (especially science, history, or English).

The more extensive and difficult the information you need to understand, the more complex your pictorial summary may have to be. Rearranging information in this way will not only show connections you may have missed but also help you understand them better. It sure makes review easier!

Add a vocabulary list

Many questions on exams require students to define the terminology in a discipline. Your physics professor will want to know what vectors are, while your calculus teacher will want to know about differential equations. Your history professor will want you to be well-versed on the Cold War, and your English literature professor will require you to know about the Romantic Poets.

Therefore, as I read my textbooks, I was sure to write down all new terms and definitions in my notes and draw little boxes around them, because I knew these were among the most likely items to be asked about on tests, and that the boxes would always draw my attention to them when I was reviewing.

Most textbooks will provide definitions of key terms. If your textbook does *not* define a key term, however, make sure that you write the term down in your notes *with its definition*. Remember that your notes should reflect *your* individual understanding of the term. Take the time to rephrase and write it in your own words. This will help you remember it.

Wait, you're not done yet!

After you've finished making notes on a chapter, go through them and identify the most important points—the ones that might turn up on tests—either with an asterisk or by highlighting them. You'll probably end up marking about 40 or 50 percent of your entries.

When you're reviewing for a test, you should read all the notes, but your asterisks will indicate which points you considered the most important _while the chapter was fresh in your mind._

To summarize, when it comes to taking notes from your texts or other reading material, you should:

- Take a cursory look through the chapter _before_ you begin reading. Look for subheads, highlighted terms, and summaries at the end of the chapter to give you a sense of the content.

- Read each section thoroughly. While your review of the chapter "clues" will help you to understand the material, you should read for comprehension rather than speed.

- Make notes immediately after you've finished reading, using the outline, time line, concept tree, and vocabulary list methods of organization as necessary.

- Mark with an asterisk or highlight the key points as you review your notes.

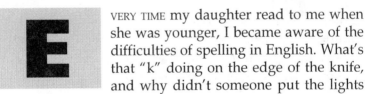

CHAPTER 7

Rembring How too Spel Gud

VERY TIME my daughter read to me when she was younger, I became aware of the difficulties of spelling in English. What's that "k" doing on the edge of the knife, and why didn't someone put the lights out on that "gh" in night? How come graffiti has two "f's" and one "t" while spaghetti doubles the "t" (and pronounces the "gh" as a hard "g"!)?

Well, one way to win the spelling bee in your town is to have a great vocabulary, using some of the suggestions mentioned in Chapter 5. Another way is to learn the rules of English spelling, then note the rather frequent exceptions to those rules.

Double or nothing

Many people make mistakes on words with doubled consonants. The most common quick-repeating consonants are "l," "n," "p," and "s," but "t" and "r" repeat fairly often, too. Although the incidence of these doubles might seem accidental or arbitrary, they usually follow these rules:

Double "l's" usually result from adding suffixes ending in "l" to roots beginning with the letter, vice versa for suffixes (examples: *alliterative, unusually*). However, alien does *not* have a double "l" because it is itself a root.

Double "n's" usually result from adding a suffix that turns an adjective ending in "n" into a noun (*wantonness* or *thinness*) or "-ny," which turns a noun ending in "n" into an adjective (*funny*).

Double "p's," "r's," and "s's" don't generally have a hard-and-fast rule, so you'll usually have to rely on other tricks of memory. For instance, I've always had trouble spelling *embarrassment* (double "r" *and* double "s") because it certainly doesn't seem to follow the same rule as *harassment* (double "s" only).

Double "r's" and double "t's" and other doubles occurring (note the double "r"!) before "-ed":

1. If the word ends in a single consonant (occuR, omiT).
2. If the word is accented on the last syllable (comPEL, reMIT).

Is it "i" before "e" or...?

The general rule is: "I" before "e" except after "c" or when it sounds like "a," as in neighbor and weigh. This rule holds, with some exceptions: *seize, leisure, caffeine,* and the names of other chemical compounds.

Honest "-able"

Many people get thrown over words ending in "e" that have "-able" or "-ible" added to them. What to do with that final "e"? Well, here are some rules:

✎ *Keep the final "e"* for words ending in "-ice," "-ace" or "-ge." Someone is embracEABLE and situations are managEABLE.

✎ *Drop that final "e"* when it is preceded by any consonant other than "c" or "g" (*unlovable*).

Other rules for adding suffixes to words ending in "e":

✎ Retain the "e" when adding "-ly" and "-ment" (unless the word ends in "-dge." It's *judgment*, *not* judgEment).

✎ Drop the "e" before adding "y" as a suffix (*phony*).

✎ Drop the final "e" and add "-ible" to words ending in "-nce," "-uce," or "-rce" (*producible*, *unconvincible*).

✎ Use "-ible" for words ending in "-miss" (*dismissible*).

It's important to know its place

"Its" is the possessive of something (for example, its color); "it's" is used in place of "it is" or "it was" (for example, it's easy).

Now you're ready for your test

"You're" is used in place of "you are" (for example, you're tall); "your" is the adjective (for example, your grades).

Whose stuff is it anyway?

If something belongs to each person, each person's name gets the "'s" (for example, Jodi's and Dave's clothes, because they each have their own clothes), but if something belongs to people collectively, only the name closest to that something gets the "'s" (for example, Jodi and Dave's house, because the house belongs to both of them).

Affect the effect

The general rule of thumb is that affect is a verb and effect is a noun. Because rules are made to be broken, though, effect is sometimes used as a verb.

Rules are meant to be broken

The English language is based on Celtic, Norwegian, German, Latin, French, and several other languages. As a result, it veers from the rules fairly often. So, while these guidelines certainly will help you a great deal, sometimes you will have to rely on association and some of the other methods we spoke of in other chapters to remember all the *exceptions* to them.

CHAPTER 8

Remembering Numbers the Mnemonic Way

P UNTIL NOW, we've been dealing in the rich world of words. Anything having to do with words is a relatively easy task for the memory because words can always be associated with *things*, which, because they can be seen, touched, heard, and smelled, can carry more than one association and, therefore, be easier to remember.

But a number is an abstraction. Unless associated with something, it is relatively difficult to remember. For instance, most people have tremendous difficulty remembering telephone numbers that they've only heard once. The reason is that a phone number doesn't usually conjure up an image or a sensation. It is merely a bunch of digits without a relationship to one another or to you.

The trick, then, is to establish more associations for numbers.

But how? After all, they can be so abstract. It would be like trying to remember colors without having the benefit of *things* associated with those colors.

Making friends with numbers

Numbers are infinite, but the system we use to designate them is even more user-friendly than the alphabet. It consists of 10 digits that all of you should know by now (just follow the bouncing ball): 0, 1, 2, 3, 4, 5, 6, 7, 8, and 9.

The trick to the mnemonic alphabet—a rather popular technique for remembering numbers—is turning those numbers into the equivalent of letters, symbols that represent sounds. The pioneer of this concept is Harry Lorayne, author of many books on memory. His method calls for associating the 10 familiar Arabic numerals with a sound or a related group of sounds.

Here's how this brilliantly simple scheme works:

1 = T, D
2 = N
3 = M
4 = R
5 = L
6 = J, soft G, CH, SH
7 = K, hard C, hard G, Q
8 = F, V, PH
9 = P, B
0 = Z, soft C, S

You're probably thinking, "What sense does this all make, and how in heck am I supposed to remember it?"

Well, though this seems like madness, believe me, there's some extraordinarily wonderful method in it.

The number one is a single downstroke, as is the letter "T." "D" is a suitable substitute because it is pronounced almost the same way as "T" — by touching the tongue to the front of the roof of the mouth.

"N" represents two because "N" has two downstrokes.

"M" is a stand-in for three because, you guessed it, it has three downstrokes.

Four is represented by "R" because the dominant sound in the word *four* is the "-RRRRRR" at the end.

The Romans used "L" to represent 50. Also, if you fan out the fingers of your left hand as if to say, "It's 5 o'clock," your index finger and thumb form the letter "L."

Hold a mirror up to a six and you get a "J," particularly if you write as badly as I do. Therefore, all letters pronounced like "J" — by touching your tongue to the inside of your lower teeth — are acceptable substitutes for six.

Place two sevens back to back, turning one upside down, and what do you have? Right, a "K." All of those letter sounds formed in the back of the mouth, as is "K," are therefore potential substitutes for the lucky seven.

Draw a line parallel to the ground through a handwritten eight and you will create a symbol that resembles a script, lower case "F." Therefore, all sounds formed by placing the top teeth on the lower lip can represent eight.

Once again, I invoke my mirror, mirror on the wall to show that a nine and a capital "P" are virtually identical. "B," also formed by putting your lips together, is a substitute for nine anytime.

Zero is an easy one. Zero begins with a "Z," so any sound formed by hissing through the space between flat tongue and roof of mouth is acceptable.

Lorayne reminds us that what's important is the *sounds* these letters make. That's why, when using mnemonics, you assign no numerical value to silent letters nor to doubled consonants (two "tt's" is the same sound as one), unless each of the letters *sounds* differently (for example, accessory).

Now what?

Believe me, the mnemonic alphabet, which probably seems very ungainly to you now, is a terrific way to remember numbers. Go over the list on page 90 a few more times, cover it up, and take the little quiz below, matching numbers with appropriate sounds and vice-versa:

8_____
V_____
N_____
3_____
T_____
K_____
7_____
R_____
P_____
0_____

Consonantal divide

Have you noticed that all of the sounds used in the mnemonic alphabet are consonants? That's because users of the system are free to use vowels however they please around these consonants to form words or memorable sounds. Therefore the number 85 can be FooL. Or the number of that wonderful person you met in the student union today and would so like to see again could be a "normal girl," or 243-5475 (NRMLGRL).

How about trying to remember pi to seven places. You could try to memorize 3.141592 or think, "MeTRic TalL PeNny."

Is it easier to remember your social security number (say, 143-25-7170) or "DooRMeN LiKe DoGS"?

A great date

One of the most useful applications of this method is remembering dates and tying them to events. If you wanted to remember, for example, William the Conqueror invaded England in 1066, you could endlessly repeat that sentence, or you could remember, "Bill THiS eGG." Combining these methods with the chain-link technique we discussed in earlier chapters, you could imagine an egg rolling off the white cliffs of Dover, where William first landed. (Alternately, you can make up a ridiculous but simple rhyme like, "In 1066, Billy C ate fish and chips" — that would also work just fine.)

Now you try it. Make up phrases using the mnemonic alphabet equivalents for your Social Security number, the first three phone numbers in your little black book, or the times for high and low tide tomorrow. Then try the quiz, writing in first the letter equivalents for the numbers, then a brief word, phrase, or sentence that would help you remember it. I've done the first one for you.

633020	JMMSNS	JiMMy'S NoSe
489306	_____	
57839462	_____	
925587025	_____	
1234567890	_____	
8951204736	_____	

What about even longer numbers? How do you remember 20-, 30-, even 50-digit numbers without trying too hard? Well, you could make your "story sentences" longer. But you can also group the numbers into a series of pictures. For example, let's say you had to remember the number 168758832427799418509079855088 — that's 30 digits! Try grouping it into smaller number combinations, creating a picture for each.

- ✎ 1687588 represents The eDGe oF a CLiFF.
- ✎ 3242779 is MNRNGCP. Standing there is a MaN weaRiNG a CaP. (Do you see him?)
- ✎ 9418509 is BRDFLSB. A BiRD FLieS By. What happens next?
- ✎ 079855088 is HSCPFLLSFF. HiS CaP FaLLS oFF.

Can you see how you could easily memorize a 50-digit number with just four or five pictures? Try it yourself. You'll see how easy it is.

Everybody loves them dead presidents

Or so sang bluesman Willie Dixon, referring to the presidential portraits that grace our folding money. But he could just as easily have been referring to your least favorite history professor — you know, the one who expects you to know who the 23rd president of the United States was? By the way, that was Harrison, and the way we will remember that is "No ('N' represents 2), My ('M' is for 3) hairy son."

Now you try it. Here are a dozen pretty obscure U.S. vice presidents. How are you going to remember them?

11. George Dallas
12. Millard Fillmore
13. William King
14. John Breckinridge
15. Hannibal Hamlin
16. Andrew Johnson
17. Schuyler Colfax
18. Henry Wilson
19. William Wheeler
20. Chester Arthur
21. Thomas Hendricks
22. Levi Morton

How did you do?

Here's how I would use mnemonics to establish a chain link between names and numbers:

- ✎ A DoMe was built to honor the king. (13)
- ✎ The Johnsons have a DitCH in their backyard. (16)
- ✎ Will's son is DeaF. (18)
- ✎ Imagine having arthritis (Arthur) in your NoSe. (20)

Get the idea? This is an absolutely invaluable tool. It will empower you to remember phone numbers without resorting to writing on wet cocktail napkins. Perhaps more important, it will help you remember dates and facts without incessantly repeating them.

Where to hang your memory

Another mnemonic memory method is the Peg Word System, which assigns a different word to numbers one through 10 (and, as Harry Lorayne describes in many of his books, can be extended right up to 100). Harry's peg words don't need to be memorized because they're based on the mnemonic alphabet you already learned:

1. Tie
2. Noah
3. Ma
4. Rye
5. Law
6. Shoe
7. Cow
8. Ivy
9. Bee
10. Toes

When you have to remember a list *in order* or associate a number with some other information (such as vice presidents of the United States), you can use these peg words for the numbers. And as I said above, Harry has even extended the list to 100, utilizing words such as mummy (33), cage (76), roof (48), and dozes (100).

It's certainly possible to create your own peg word system utilizing the sounds of the mnemonic alphabet (though why reinvent the wheel Harry already designed?). Alternatively, you can utilize a completely different basic peg word system cited by author Dr. Fiona McPherson in her book *The Memory Key* (Career Press, 2000). While not associating it to the sounds used in the mnemonic alphabet, using a rhyme scheme makes it equally memorable: "One is a bun, two is a shoe, three is a tree, four is a door, five is a hive, six is sticks, seven is heaven, eight is a gate, nine is a line, and ten is a hen."

As I emphasize throughout this book, use whichever method or list of peg words you find easiest, or create your own!

CHAPTER 9

Remembering Names and Faces

IKE IT OR not, you're not going to be in school for the rest of your life. Soon, you will begin to look for a job, to string together a network of acquaintances and contacts that will help lift you onto that first rung of the corporate ladder.

You'll participate in that horrible convention called the cocktail party and other social events where you'll be expected to be charming.

Every once in a while, I go to a cocktail party, if only to remind myself why I don't do it more often. But seriously, cocktail parties give me a chance to practice a skill that I consider one of the key reasons for my earlier success as an advertising salesperson: remembering the names (and some of the other pertinent personal data) that go with the faces.

In fact, one of the principal reasons I became interested in the subject of memory improvement was that I was tired of calling people "pal" and "buddy" when I could *not* remember their names after they said to *me,* "Hey, Ron, how have you been?"

If you have as much trouble remembering names and faces as I did, don't think you're unique. Studies have shown that of the 13 memory tasks people are most commonly concerned about (from remembering important dates, where you've put something, or whether you've done something to remembering what you've read or studied), *four* of them relate to identity: remembering someone's name when you see their face; being able to picture a face when you know a name; remembering facts about someone you've met (their profession, children's names, spouse's name); and associating a person with a context (knowing that the person in front of you, whose name you actually remember, is the local baker).

The following techniques will help you avoid those embarrassing cocktail party gaffes ("Oh, yeah, I *meant* to call you George even though I *know* your name is Samantha.") by showing you how to link any number of names, faces, and "vital characteristics" in a story or series of pictures.

Take a good look

Whenever you meet someone, look him or her in the face and make special note of some outstanding feature. Does the person have a big nose? Huge earlobes? Dimples? Big, beautiful blue eyes? A cleft in the chin? A mole? It doesn't have to be a particularly ugly or beautiful feature—just something that sets the person apart from the rest of the people in the room.

Once you've locked in on a feature, *don't* stare at it, but *do* get your imagination working—make that feature truly outstanding by embellishing it. If it's a big nose, make it as big as a toucan's beak in your mind's eye. Dimples should be as large as craters; big earlobes should dangle on the person's shoulders.

Don't feel you have to use this technique on every person you see; it's still easier to utilize obvious clues to jog your memory. Do you see the person's spouse at the party? Remember *his* name? *Voila!* Suddenly you remember *her* name. Recognize someone but can't figure out why? Instead of concentrating on the person or his or her face, think about *where* you know them from. We remember people in specific contexts and may have a difficult time if we meet them outside of that context. You may have had the same guy fill your gas tank every week for months but get confused if you suddenly see him at a baseball game. Once you remember he works at the gas station, you'll probably remember his name!

Make sure you got it

I remember once introducing my friend Tony to three people who, along with him, were the first to arrive at my house for a dinner party. One minute later, I went into the kitchen to fix drinks for everybody and Tony was right at my heels. "What was the name of that brunette in the miniskirt?" he asked in a hushed voice. "Monique," I said. "How 'bout the bald guy?" asked Tony. "That's Joe." Finally, very embarrassed, Tony asked, "And what about the other woman?"

There are fleas with longer memories. But now Tony prides himself on being able to remember the names of 30 or 40 people in a room after being introduced only once.

The first thing he taught himself to do was to repeat the person's name, looking right at him or her as he did so. Tony, being a very charming guy, doesn't do this as if he's trying out for a lead role in the remake of *Being There*. He repeats the name back as part of a greeting—"Nice to meet you,

Monique." "Hi Joe, I've heard a lot about you. You're Ron's partner, right?"

Using such a technique, you will not only be noting the person's name, you will be making sure that you got it right.

Think of a link

Once you've done that, it's time to come up with some sort of link between the name and the feature that you've already exaggerated out of proportion.

I saw the most obvious example of this as a kid when a memorist appeared on a Sunday morning TV show. He was introduced to the 100 or so youngsters in the audience and repeated all of their names back to them at the end of the show. Asked how he had done it, he used the example of a boy named Tommy Fox. The boy had a dimple, said the memorist, so he imagined a bare meadow with a hole in the middle. A fox bounded through the hedge followed by hunters shouting, "Tommy Ho!"

Bingo! The name and the face were linked forever.

Too easy, you say?

There are much *easier* ones. Before you go too far afield creating a memorable mental picture, don't overlook the obvious. Some names are so memorable you shouldn't have to work too hard—try "Boomer" Esiason (okay, you *might* have to work on "Esiason") or Chip Dale (gotta love those chipmunks). Other first or last names should *automatically* trigger specific pictures—a flower (Rose, Daisy, Hyacinth), a piece of jewelry (Amber, Ruby, Jasper, Opal, Pearl, Jade, Ivory), an object (Gates, Ford, Bentley, Royce, Zipper, Glass, Cross, Brook, River, Pen, Pack, Beam, Tent, *ad infinitum*), a profession (Tinker, Taylor, Soldier, Spy), a city or town (Clifton, Springfield, Austin, Houston, Dallas, Savannah,

York), a familiar street, the name of your favorite team, a breed of dog or cat.

Some names differing by only a letter could use such objects as links—Pack to remember Gregory *Peck*, Pen for Sean *Penn*, Tent for *Trent*, Road for *Rhodes* or, for a little more stretch, Tombs for *Thomas*, Cow for *Cowher* (Go, Steelers!).

Your associations could take advantage of your own particular knowledge. Small for *Klein*, if you know German; tie-ins to your favorite sports figure, movie star, or author; an association with terms endemic to your profession. The list of possible tie-ins is absolutely endless.

If you *still* can't think of such a link, you can always rhyme: Wallets for *Wallace*, Georgie Porgie, Bad Chad, Freaky Frank, Ron weighs a ton.

Once you've come up with these soundalikes or pictures, find some way to link them with the image you've formed of the person's chief facial features.

For instance, once I was introduced to a man named Vince Dolce (pronounced Dole-see). As I was walking toward him, I noticed some rather dark circles under his eyes. In my imagination, because I'm so accustomed to using the technique outlined above, the circles became bigger than a raccoon's. When I heard that his name was Dolce, I immediately thought, "dull sheep" and pictured tired, sleepy sheep grazing on those now even bigger circles below Vince's eyes. The sheep, of course, were bothering him, and this made him *wince* (for Vince).

That's all there is to turning a room full of strangers into people that—for better or worse—you'll never forget!

CHAPTER 10

Let's Not Forget ADD

E MUST FACE and deal with what's happening to the three million-plus kids who are on a legal drug—Ritalin, the prescribed drug of choice for those diagnosed with Attention Deficit Disorder (ADD), hyperactivity, or the combination of the two (ADHD). I could write a book on ADD, which seems to be the "diagnosis of choice" for school kids these days.

Luckily, I don't have to. Thom Hartmann has already written an excellent one—*Attention Deficit Disorder: A Different Perception*—from which I have freely and liberally borrowed (with his permission) for this chapter.

I'm going to have to leave others to debate whether ADD actually exists as a clearly definable illness, whether it's the "catchall" diagnosis of lazy doctors, whether teachers are labeling kids as ADD to avoid taking responsibility for students' poor learning skills, whether Ritalin is a miracle drug or one that is medicating creative kids into a conforming stupor.

All of these positions *have* been asserted and, as hundreds of new kids are medicated every day, the debate about ADD is only likely to continue...and heat up. That is not my concern in this book.

What I want to deal with here is the reality that many kids, however they're labeled, have severe problems in dealing with school as it usually exists. I want to give them the advice they need to contend with the symptoms that have acquired the label "ADD."

Some definitions, please

Just what is ADD? It's probably easiest to describe as a person's difficulty focusing on a simple thing for any significant amount of time. People with ADD are described as easily distracted, impatient, impulsive, and often seeking immediate gratification. They have poor listening skills and have trouble doing "boring" jobs (like sitting quietly in class or, as adults, balancing a checkbook). "Disorganized" and "messy" are words that also come up often.

Hyperactivity is more clearly defined as restlessness, resulting in excessive activity. Hyperactives are usually described as having "ants in their pants." ADHD, the first category recognized in medicine some 75 years ago, is a combination of hyperactivity and ADD.

According to the American Psychiatric Association, a person has ADHD if he or she meets eight or more of the following paraphrased criteria:

1. Can't remain seated if required to do so.
2. Easily distracted by extraneous stimuli.

3. Focusing on a single task or play activity is difficult.
4. Frequently begins another activity without completing the first.
5. Fidgets or squirms (or feels restless mentally).
6. Can't (or doesn't want to) wait for his turn during group activities.
7. Will often interrupt with an answer before a question is completed.
8. Has problems with chore or job follow-through.
9. Can't play quietly easily.
10. Impulsively jumps into physically dangerous activities without weighing the consequences.
11. Easily loses things (pencils, tools, papers) necessary to complete school or work projects.
12. Interrupts others inappropriately.
13. Talks impulsively or excessively.
14. Doesn't seem to listen when spoken to.

Three caveats to keep in mind: The behaviors must have started before age 7, not represent some other form of classifiable mental illness, and occur more frequently than in the average person of the same age.

Characteristics of people with ADD

Let's look at the characteristics generally ascribed to people with ADD in more detail:

Easily distracted. Because ADD people are constantly "scoping out" everything around them, focusing on a single item is difficult. Just try having a conversation with an ADD person while a television is on.

Short, but very intense, attention span. Though it can't be defined in terms of minutes or hours, anything ADD people find boring immediately loses their attention. Other projects may hold their rapt and extraordinarily intense attention for hours or days.

Disorganization. ADD children are often chronically disorganized — their rooms are messy, their desks are a shambles, their files incoherent. While people without ADD can be equally messy and disorganized, they can usually find what they are looking for; ADDers *can't*.

Distortions of time-sense. ADDers have an exaggerated sense of urgency when they're working on something and an exaggerated sense of boredom when they have nothing interesting to do.

Difficulty following directions. A new theory on this aspect holds that ADDers have difficulty processing auditory or verbal information. A major aspect of this difficulty involves the very-common reports of parents of ADD kids who say their kids love to watch TV and hate to read.

Daydreaming, falling into depressions, or having mood swings.

Take risks. ADDers seem to make faster decisions than non-ADDers. This is why Thom Hartmann and Wilson Harrell, former publisher of *Inc.* magazine and author of *For Entrepreneurs Only*, conclude the vast majority of successful entrepreneurs probably have ADD! They call them "Hunters," as opposed to the more staid "Farmer" types.

Easily frustrated and impatient. ADDers do not suffer fools gladly. They are direct and to-the-point. When things aren't working, "Do something!" is the ADD rallying cry, even if that something is a bad idea.

Why ADD kids have trouble in school

First and foremost, says Thom Hartmann, schools are set up for "farmers" — sit at a desk, do what you're told, watch and listen to the teacher. This is pure hell for the "hunters" with ADD. The bigger the class size, the worse it becomes. Kids with ADD, remember, are easily distracted, bored, turned off, always ready to move on.

What should you look for in a school setting to make it more palatable to an ADD son or daughter? What can you do at home to help your child (or yourself)? Hartmann has some solid answers.

 Learning needs to be project- and experience-based, providing more opportunities for creativity and shorter and smaller "bites" of information. Many "gifted" programs offer exactly such opportunities. The problem for many kids with ADD is that they've spent years in nongifted, farmer-type classroom settings and may be labeled with underachieving behavior problems, effectively shut out of the programs virtually designed for them! Many parents report that children diagnosed as ADD, who failed miserably in public school, thrived in private school. Hartmann attributes this to the smaller classrooms, more individual attention with specific goal-setting, project-based learning, and similar methods common in such schools. These factors are just what make ADD kids thrive!

Create a weekly performance template on which _both_ teacher and parent chart the child's performance, positive and negative. "Creating such a larger-than-the-child system," claims Hartmann, "will help keep ADD children on task and on time."

Encourage special projects for extra credit. Projects give ADDers the chance to learn in the mode that's most appropriate for them. They will also give such kids the chance to make up for the "boring" homework they sometimes simply can't make themselves do.

✎ **Stop labeling them "disordered."** Kids react to labels, especially negative ones, even more than adults. Saying "you have a deficit and a disorder" may be more destructive than useful.

✎ **Think twice about medication,** but don't discard the option. Hartmann has a concern about the long-term side effects of drugs normally prescribed for ADDers. He notes that they may well be more at risk to be substance abusers as adults, so starting them on medication at a young age sends a very mixed message. However, if an ADD child cannot have his or her special needs met in a classroom, *not* medicating him or her may be a disaster. "The relatively unknown long-term risks of drug therapy," says Hartmann, "may be more than offset by the short-term benefits of improved classroom performance."

Specific suggestions for remembering

✎ **Practice, practice, practice** the memory techniques in this book. ADDers tend to have trouble listening and are easily distracted. As a result, they may fail to remember things they simply never heard or paid attention to. Work on the visualization techniques. Practice making mental pictures when having conversations; create mental images of your "to-do" list; visualize doing things to which you've committed or for which you are receiving instructions or directions. Practice careful listening skills. Many of Harry Lorayne's memory books (especially his classic, *The Memory Book*), which stress "picture-oriented" approaches to memory problems, would be invaluable additions to any ADDer's library.

✎ **Write everything down.** This is something I recommend everyone doing, but it is absolutely essential for ADDers. The more you write down, the less you have to remember!

✎ **Utilize pictures, mapping, diagrams,** and so on in lieu of outlines or "word" notes—even the abbreviations and shorthand I've recommended in _Take Notes_.

✎ **Tape record lectures,** despite what I wrote in _How to Study_. This will enable them to relisten and reprocess information they may have missed the first time around.

✎ **Create distraction-free zones.** Henry David Thoreau (who evidently suffered from ADD, by the way) was so desperate to escape distraction he moved to isolated Walden Pond. Have them organize their time and workspace to create their own "Walden Pond," especially when they have to write, take notes, read, or study. ADDers need silence, so consider the library. Another tip: Have them clean their work areas thoroughly at the end of each day. This will minimize distractions.

✎ **Train your attention span.** ADDers will probably never be able to train themselves to ignore distractions totally, but a variety of meditation techniques might help them stay focused longer.

CHAPTER 11

Test Your Progress

S PROMISED, I'M going to give you a chance to check your progress. If you've studied the contents of this book thoroughly and have made an effort to put some of its advice to work, you should score much higher now than you did on the quiz in Chapter 2.

Test #1: the mnemonic alphabet

Study this number for 30 seconds. Then cover it up and replicate as much as you can, taking only another 20 seconds or so.

51448569754120657205

Test #2: a better vocabulary

Here are a number of obscure vocabulary words and their meanings. Study them for no more than three minutes, then answer the questions below.

extant	not destroyed or lost
imprest	a loan
leman	mistress
panettone	Italian yeast bread made with raisins, almonds, and candied fruits
plutocracy	rule by the wealthy
discalced	barefoot
vacillating	indecisive
maraud	to raid
rusticate	to go to live in the country
albumen	the white of an egg
soporific	sleepy or drowsy
claque	a group hired to applaud an act or performer
damson	a small, dark blue plum
pollex	thumb
eristic	pertaining to controversy
wunderkind	a child prodigy
eruct	to belch
tusche	a grease-like liquid used in lithography
savarin	a sponge-like cake leavened with yeast, baked in a ring mold, often soaked with rum
umber	dark reddish brown

Okay, cover them up and take the test on the next page:

1. The plum cobbler recipe called specifically for ___.
2. Whenever my grandmother is homesick for Italy, she bakes a loaf of ___.
3. Many college graduates try to take out an ___ to pay off their credit-card debt.
4. Before democracy was popular, there was often ___, because whoever had the most money took power.
5. A type of liquid used in lithography is ___.
6. I've had enough of city life, so I'm going to ___.
7. Many people make omelettes from ___ since the yolk has so much cholesterol.
8. Another word for thumb is ___.
9. A rum-soaked cake is a ___.
10. Despite having many wives, King Henry VIII was rarely without a ___.
11. People say to avoid ___ topics during dinner, such as religion and politics.
12. Sometimes the color of soil is ___.
13. Another word for belch is ___.
14. Pirates would often ___ other ships for their treasures.
15. Doogie Howser was definitely a ___.
16. Many people take naps on Thanksgiving because there's something in turkey that supposedly makes people ___.
17. Archeologists have recovered all kinds of ___ remains from the dinosaur era.
18. I stick to decisions once I make them, but my husband doesn't; he's very ___.
19. In the summertime, many people walk around ___ because they like to feel the grass on their feet.
20. Live television shows often have a ___ in the audience in case the rest of the audience doesn't laugh or applaud.

Test #3: dates and events

Study the following dates, events, and facts. Then take the test on the next page.

✎✎✎

- ✎ In 1899, Dr. Felix Hoffman of Germany invented aspirin.
- ✎ Boston was the first U.S. city with a subway.
- ✎ John Adams and Thomas Jefferson died on the same day (July 4, 1826).
- ✎ Virginia state where the most presidents were born (8).
- ✎ The Treaty of Versailles, which ended WWI, was signed in 1919.
- ✎ In 1896, the Supreme Court, in the case of *Plessy v. Fergusen,* ruled that "separate but equal" was a constitutional philosophy for the treatment of different races.
- ✎ The Lincoln cent is the only circulating coin currently produced in which the portrait faces to the right.
- ✎ Diabetes is the leading cause of blindness in people ages 20-74.
- ✎ February 18th is Pluto Day, the anniversary of its discovery in 1930.
- ✎ Theodore Geisel (a.k.a. Dr. Seuss) was born in Springfield, MA in 1904.
- ✎ The state motto of Illinois is "State sovereignty — national union."
- ✎ The modern Olympic Games first held in Athens, Greece in 1896.
- ✎ FBI's "10 Most Wanted Fugitives" program begins in March of 1950 .
- ✎ The American Medical Association was organized in 1847.

Now answer the following questions:

1. Which war did the Treaty of Versailles end and when was it signed?
2. What is the leading cause of blindness in people ages 20-74?
3. When and where was Dr. Seuss born?
4. What is the only circulating coin currently produced with the portrait facing right?
5. When was Pluto discovered?
6. When was the AMA organized?
7. What did Dr. Felix Hoffman invent in 1899?
8. What Supreme Court case ruled that "separate but equal" was constitutional?
9. When did the FBI's "10 Most Wanted" program begin?
10. What was the first U.S. city with a subway?
11. Where was the first modern Olympics held?
12. In which state were the most U.S. presidents born?
13. What is the state motto of Illinois?
14. Which two presidents died on the same day? What day?

Test #4: reading retention

Scan the following paragraphs excerpted from _CEO Logic_ (Career Press, 1998), in order to answer the questions that follow (which you may read first). The answers are at the end of Test 4. This should take you no more than two minutes:

A sales manager's job is both strategic and operational. It is to develop and discipline the selling system, measure and manage sales efficiency, build a sales team, define the sales message, solve day-to-day selling problems, and guide and motivate the sales force to meet their objectives. Further, her job is, like a CEO, to simultaneously be the chief skeptic and the chief optimist. As chief skeptic, the sales manager analyzes and anticipates problems.

At the same time, sales managers must also be able to generate hope, energy, and optimism in order to motivate the sales force to out enthusiastic actions behind important plans. Balancing these roles can be a delicate matter. If the skeptic role becomes too prominent, a sales force can easily be demoralized with too much gloom and doom. But being overly optimistic and unrealistic does no good either. So the sales manager, like a CEO, must be able to manage both roles skillfully to keep the troops focused on success and performance.

1. The author links the sales manager's job with that of her ___.

    a. sales force

    b. CEO

    c. assistant

    d. co-workers

2. Which of the following is not one of the sales manager's jobs?

    a. cause problems

    b. solve day-to-day selling problems

    c. measure and manage sales efficiency

    d. build a sales team

3. A sales manager's job is to be the chief optimist and at the same time the chief ___.

    a. motivator

    b. skeptic

    c. boss

    d. negotiator

4. Which of the following adjectives does not describe a sales manager's role?

    a. strategic

    b. developmental

    c. friendly

    d. operational

Now read the following passage and answer the questions that follow (but do not look at the questions first). Give yourself four minutes for this exercise:

Abdollah Nouri does not look like a dangerous counter-revolutionary. In a nation run by clerics, he ranks among the most senior, not quite an ayatullah but a *hojatolislam*, or "proof of Islam." His outspokenness is one reason the powers that be in Iran wish to destroy him.

This week Nouri will be called before a court to answer a 44-page indictment. He stands accused of dishonoring the Ayatullah Khomeini, undermining the authority of Iran's ruling clergy, and promoting relations with the U.S. If he is convicted, he faces a hefty fine, lashes of the whip, or a dozen years in prison. Much more critically, Nouri will then be disqualified from heading the reform ticket in next

February's elections, thus ending any chance of his becoming the powerful speaker of Iran's 270-seat parliament, the Majlis-e-Shura. A victory by Nouri is crucial to his chief ally, the embattled reformist President of Iran, Mohammed Khatami, and his efforts to promote moderation, expand freedom, and normalize Iran's relations with the outside world.

This is not Nouri's first scuffle with hard-liners: In an impeachment trial last year, parliament ousted him as Minister of the Interior for permitting student demonstrations. Since then, his main vehicle of dissent has been the national daily *Khordad*. The newspaper has published antiregime opinions by prominent clerics, notably Grand Ayatullah Hossein Ali Montazeri, who has been under house arrest since 1997 for questioning *velayat-e-faqih*, the absolute authority of the clergy.

Being the patron and publisher of such notions has made Nouri one of the most popular politicians in Iran. [Khatami's] strategy is to send a flood of loyalist candidates to the election board, so that even if political stars like Nouri are barred, a solid number will survive the vetting process and get elected. Nouri praises Khatami for making government more accountable but warns that the President's program will face "serious problems" if reform forces are unfairly excluded from the next parliament.

1. Does parliament support personal freedoms?
2. Do President Khatami and the Majlis-e-Shura have similar political views?

Neither of these answers are directly stated in the selection, though both can be easily inferred from it. The answers are: 1) No, because the parliament impeached Nouri for allowing student demonstrations; and 2) No. Noiri is a chief ally to Khatami, but the Majlis-e-Shura stripped Nouri of his position as Minister of the Interior.

Answers to the first part of Test 4

1. b   3. b
2. a   4. c

Test #5: remembering even obscure lists

Study the first two lists for one minute each, then close the book and recite them back. Do the same for the third and fourth lists, except allow three minutes for the third, five minutes for the fourth:

Civil War battles: Bentonville, Fort Fisher, Pea Ridge, Sparta, Corinth, Shiloh, New Berne, Chickamauga, Iuka, Trevilian Station, Monocacy.

Birds: Pacific loon, eared grebe, short-tailed shearwater, white ibis, wood stork, snow goose, gadwall, sora, whimbrel, mourning dove, sky lark, oliva sparrow, boboink.

Music: merengue, mariachi, jungle, dixieland, bluegrass, celtic, Eurodance, Gothic, industrial, reggae, freestyle, ragtime, vallenato, trance, tejano, illbient, house, skiffle, bhangra, bossa nova, andean, dub.

Ships or vessels: Monoxylon, drake, whiff, packet, lymphad, galley, carrack, bawley, praam, randan, sub, razee, geordie, felucca, bireme, coracle, dinghy, skiff, sloop, grab, coaster, brigantine, saic, tern, tub, tug, fore-and-after, masoolah, puteli, shallop, patamar, gallivat, dogger, gondola, butty, budgerow.

Test #6: the rules of English spelling

Identify the misspelled words in the following list:

✎✎✎

- [ ] embarrass
- [ ] supercede
- [ ] parallell
- [ ] penicillin
- [ ] livlihood
- [ ] posess
- [ ] independent
- [ ] reccomend
- [ ] accommodate
- [ ] correspondance
- [ ] dilemma
- [ ] comparitive
- [ ] occurrance
- [ ] likable
- [ ] seperate

✎✎✎

How did you do? (See the bottom of the page for the spelling solutions.)

I hope that you scored well and are confident that you can approach your schoolwork—and the rest of your life, inside and outside of school—with the assurance that your memory will be an ally rather than a foil.

In the previous list, the following are the only words spelled *correctly:* embarrass, penicillin, independent, accommodate, and dilemma.

Index

F

H

I

K

L

M

N

NOTES

NOTES

NOTES